TRAIN LIKE YOU FLY

A FLIGHT INSTRUCTOR'S GUIDE TO SCENARIO-BASED TRAINING

Arlynn McMahon

Aviation Supplies & Academics, Inc.
Newcastle, Washington

Train Like You Fly: A flight instructor's guide to scenario-based training
by Arlynn McMahon

Aviation Supplies & Academics, Inc.
7005 132nd Place SE • Newcastle, WA 98059
Website: www.asa2fly.com • Email: asa@asa2fly.com

Printed in the United States of America

2011   2010   9 8 7 6 5 4 3 2

Illustrations, tables, and photo credits: Table 2-2 on p. 23 and Diversion Exercise tables pp. 30-37 adapted from email exchanges with David Hunter; Page 49 "sample FITS Lesson Plan" adapted from FITS Master Instructor Syllabus; all photographs © Arlynn McMahon except p.134 © Stephanie Phillips and p. 56 © Mark Anders.

Cover runway photo © Paul Kine

ASA-TRAIN-FLY
ISBN 1-56027-707-6
     978-1-56027-707-1

Library of Congress Cataloging-in-Publication Data:
McMahon, Arlynn.
   Train like you fly : a flight instructor's guide to scenario-based training / by Arlynn McMahon.
       p. cm.

   Includes bibliographical references.
   1. Flight training. 2. Teachers--Training of. 3. Example. I. Title.

TL712.M395 2008
629.132'52071--dc22   2008022206

Arlynn McMahon began her love of aviation as a youngster. She soloed on her 16th birthday; since that time her feet have rarely been on the ground. Arlynn is a graduate of Aero-Tech of Lexington, Kentucky, and also a graduate of Embry-Riddle Aeronautical University.

Arlynn has helped more than 1,000 students and CFIs fulfill their dreams of flight since she joined Aero-Tech as an instructor in 1984. A career flight instructor, she recently completed a MBA in Strategic Leadership from Amberton University. Today she serves as Aero-Tech's Vice President and Training Centers Manager, responsible for all pilot training and flight activities. She is an active FAA Accident Prevention Counselor and was the 1991 FAA Regional Flight Instructor of the Year. Arlynn specializes in teaching Aeronautical Decision-Making and Cockpit-Risk Management to the aircraft owner/nonprofessional pilot. She is a guest speaker at many aviation safety seminars and functions.

Arlynn possesses an Airline Transport Pilot for multi-engine privileges and a Commercial Pilot Certificate for single engine privileges. She is a FAA Gold Seal and NAFI Master Instructor, with CFI, CFII, MEI, AGI, and over 10,000 accident-free hours, including 7,000 hours dual given. She is a Designated Sport Pilot Examiner and a FAAST Representative.

In 2006 Arlynn married her flight instructor and best friend, Charlie Monette. When not in a cockpit, they share sailing, scuba diving and all types of fun in the sun.

2

Contents

Chapter Three: Syllabus Redesign

Chapter Four: Debriefing and Evaluating

Chapter Five: Instrument Scenario Training

Chapter Six: Scenarios for Advanced Training

Chapter Seven: Scenarios for Flight Instructor Training

Chapter Eight: Weather in Scenarios

Chapter Nine: The Right Attitude

Chapter Ten: Wisdom Report Scenarios

Chapter Eleven: Gold Standards for Employees

Chapter Twelve: Designing Your Own Scenarios

Chapter Thirteen: Why Bother Using Scenarios to Train Pilots?

Radio-Call Pilot Aid

Section Chart Excerpts for Chapter 2 Diversion Exercise Scenarios (close-up versions)

Learning Plateau Game Sheet

Glossary

IFR General NTSB Reports

Bibliography and Internet References

Footnotes by Chapter

Foreword

What are FITS, SBT, and SRM? These questions are beginning to be asked by the general aviation (GA) instructor community. *Train Like You Fly* answers these questions and provides guidance to instructors and training managers on how to effectively teach judgment and decision-making in GA flight training. It identifies "learning moments" where both student and expert pilots can develop, practice, and rehearse their judgment and decision-making skills.

The aviation community readily recognizes the need for an improvement in GA safety of at least one order of magnitude. The high accident rate that emerged with the introduction of the technically advanced aircraft (TAA) has caused the aviation community to question the safety of the aircraft and the new technology. A closer look at TAA accidents has revealed that pilots are crashing good airplanes with fully functional equipment. The common thread in these accidents as well as 75 to 80% of all GA accidents is human factors, or what is usually called "pilot error." These accidents are either caused by, or have contributing factors related to bad judgment or incorrect decisions.

These discoveries have led to a safety initiative that aims to resolve these problems among general aviation pilots. The safety initiative, FAA/Industry Training Standards (FITS), is a joint FAA, industry, and academic accord that examines best practices both outside and within the aviation training community. The result of this safety initiative has been the development and implementation of the FITS tenets. The tenets include scenario-based training (SBT), learner centered grading, and single-pilot resource management (SRM). Three independent studies by the FITS research team found significant improvements in several measurements of pilot performance—situational awareness, and aeronautical decision-making. This book provides a practical guide to training managers and instructors for using FITS tenets in GA flight training.

Unfortunately, the FITS approach does not have the rich assortment of teaching techniques and teaching activities that traditional flight training has. It also does not share the luxury of having instructors who have experienced the FITS approach in their own training. Arlynn McMahon's book bridges the gap between these two approaches and guides readers through the transition to scenario-based training. Until an assortment of scenarios becomes available, training managers and individual flight instructors will need to develop their own and devise scenarios that meet specific training needs. This book provides the guidance needed to embrace the tenets of FITS.

Train Like You Fly begins with an explanation of the scenario-based training concept, and then moves into teaching pilots to think, and the debriefing and evaluation process. Many instructors will say they are already using scenarios in their instruction. Yet this book explains how simply framing the conditions where a simulated malfunction has occurred is not enough because learning a "canned" response does not teach the pilot to think critically, nor does it teach the pilot how to respond to the same malfunction under different conditions.

This book was written for flight managers and instructors. It is not a book that preaches at you, nor one that takes the abstract high ground. Rather, it recognizes your likely expertise and offers concrete advice, based on evidence, and resources upon which you can reflect. My hope is that you and your students will benefit.

Charles L. Robertson, Ph.D.
Co-Principal Investigator of FITS

Acknowledgments

It may seem coy to say, but this book truly could not have been written without the efforts of many people.

I dedicate this book to Charlie Monette, the flight instructor who gave me wings and who instilled in me a need to be the best. And who later married me and tolerated a new wife, distracted while completing this book— throughout our honeymoon, Thanksgiving and Christmas holidays.

I'd like to thank the many FAA and NASA scientists whose hard work is seldom recognized or appreciated in general aviation. Some will read this book and feel acknowledged, knowing that flight schools are finally "getting it." Some may read and be shocked to see how I've mutilated their examples in attempts to refashion something intended for airline into something for use in a general aviation flight school environment.

Last, I thank the many flight instructors whom I have had the opportunity to train and work with during my role as a Chief Instructor. They keep me on my toes, thinking forward, staying current and focused on the pilots who trust our school to make them safe.

Arlynn McMahon

A Note from the Author

I use the word "pilot" in lieu of "student" in consideration of the many doctors, lawyers, professionals, business owners and adult men and women who engage in flight training. They are commonly addressed as "sir" or "ma'am" in their office. I believe they deserve the same respect when paying for my service. Somehow, referring to a valued customer as a "student" seems belittling. I also recognize that some people receiving scenario-based training have already earned a pilot certificate. In this book I use "pilot" when referring to the person in training and "instructor" to refer to the person teaching. After all, we are all "students" of aviation in that pilots continue to learn well after the FAA certificate is awarded. The term "him" means "him or her." It's easier to read.

TRAIN LIKE YOU FLY

Chapter 1

Concepts

A Lesson

It is a beautiful day. The instructor begins the preflight discussion for Henry's tenth flight. "Henry, today we are flying to Panama City, Florida to look at a piece of property we want to buy near the airport. Take notes: After takeoff, you'll engage the autopilot and take me to Panama City Airport. You choose the altitude. Remember to program the GPS on the ground before takeoff. At Panama City I want you to contact the tower, enter the traffic pattern, disengage the autopilot and give me a crosswind landing. You'll choose if you wish to stop and taxi back or takeoff. We'll stay in the traffic pattern for two more landings before returning home. I'd like to have you handle everything. You decide what needs to be done and do it. Pretend I'm not there, but I am there if you need me."

What kind of a lesson is this? Is Henry's lesson one of navigation or one of takeoffs and landings? Is this a professional instructor who says to a student, you do everything and I'm not going to help you? [1]

What is a Scenario?

The lesson above requires Henry to think and practice making decisions while he is controlling the flying machine. This is a great lesson conducted by a skillful instructor who understands the issues facing today's pilots. "New cockpit technology has tended to place more importance on the pilot as an information processor, decision maker and manager."[2] Consider this an example of scenario-based training.

The scenario is a viable tool in flight training. In this chapter, the objectives, features and limitations of scenarios present a framework on which the remaining chapters of this book will be built.

We all face decisions that prove to be turning points in our lives. Sometimes we look back at that moment and feel pleased because we chose what proved to be a good decision. Other times, we later find that we missed something that, if we had only known at the time, might have yielded a different decision—and improved our future. Such is the case for too many pilots.

The scenario attempts to place the pilot in a training environment that closely reflects real flying. A scenario is "a situation." It begs the question, "You are here and this happens. How will you handle it?" In practice, scenarios resemble a set of stories, written or spoken, built around constructed plots. They apply knowledge. They allow assessment of flight skills and judgment.

Scenario-based training stems from research proving that good judgment and decision-making are teachable. Teaching pilots to think and advancing those "thinking" skills such as risk management and situational awareness are important to teaching safe piloting. Unfortunately, learning how to think is not taught in a typical course that emphasizes perfecting maneuvers. "It is assumed that they [pilots] will learn judgment through experience." [3]

Learning to operate an aircraft requires more than the ability to recite information or perform individual maneuvers. Generally pilots must use knowledge and skill together. This ability to orchestrate both knowledge and skill is a separate skill in its own right. It's the ability to think—and to think about several tasks at once—while dealing with distractions and interruptions. Thinking-skill is a skill that must be developed in every pilot.

The development of thinking-skills requires problem-solving practice. Scenarios allow the pilot to experience events, explore options and decide how to deal with the situation under the direction of an instructor. "Safety is not a natural mentality. It is one that must be developed and learned through multiple and varying experiences." [4]

The scenario may be a situation introduced in a ground briefing. For example, "What will you do after suddenly becoming aware that you haven't heard any chatter on the radio for a long while?" It may be a flight programmed into an aviation training device or it could also be a flight mission in the airplane.

Scenarios are powerful training tools precisely because the future is unpredictable. There is simply no way to train a pilot for every conceivable event that may happen in his flying future. Instructors can't foresee and orchestrate the multitude of variables that, at times, come together to create a bad day. Consequently, scenario training can be used to:

- Point to voids in understanding
- Show potential problems
- Provoke debate
- Expand the range of options that a pilot is to consider
- Apply practical application of knowledge
- Identify choices and make decisions

A scenario may represent a simple, sequential string of events. On the other hand, it may be a complex set of events, branching into new solutions. The pilot could make a decision that leads to a new and unexpected direction, perhaps diverting to another airport. Nevertheless, a good scenario is a realistic event requiring practical application of various bits of knowledge.

Features of Scenarios

The scenario presents seemingly unrelated bits of knowledge and requires the pilot to form a bigger picture. Seldom has a single event caused an aviation accident. When a situation arises, there is no flashing banner announcing "This is a weather problem" allowing the pilot to recognize it and pull the solution from a predetermined set of choices.

While instructors preach "stop the accident chain," the average pilot is not taught to recognize how multiple factors combine during flight, leading to an accident. In the real world, seemingly small problems are interlaced. Perhaps weather, terrain, regulatory, and operational considerations are involved. Thus, finding a solution to a "weather problem" with only weather-related information, without considering terrain, could result in a situation of Controlled Flight into Terrain.

A good scenario begins with a need to fly. Many times, the decisions a pilot makes are influenced by the need to fly. For example, if the pilot were delivering an organ to be transplanted into a sick child, he may take a risky flight when he otherwise would not. The scenario implies consequences—if the organ does not arrive by a certain time the child may die. This gives the pilot practice in facing challenging, real life situations that affect decisions in flight.

The construct of a scenario should not be simply "a weather scenario" or "a regulation scenario" but should be realistic in its complexity of variables. For instance:

- A good scenario is much more than an hour of flight time, it's a learning experience. Imagine experiencing the John F. Kennedy flight of reduced visibility while flying over water at night.

- A good scenario might not have one, correct answer and a good scenario does not offer the obvious answer.
- A good scenario uses all available resources: Cockpit technology, ATC, FSS, passengers, etc.
- When pilot error occurs, the pilot still must carry on, dealing with the situation as it unfolds. A good scenario does not promote errors, but should promote judgment in handling errors.
- A good scenario requires the pilot to be "in command" and to be in control of the total situation. During a scenario, the instructor is not in the role of brain-dumping knowledge onto the pilot. The instructor does not teach or coach the pilot any more than what is absolutely necessary to continue.
- Beginning with simple scenarios and moving into more complex situations, they provide a building-block manner in developing the skills of putting it all together. Some pilots may even need remedial thinking-skills training while others may be ready for complex problems.

Objectives in Scenarios

Scenarios include traditional flight maneuvers; however, the objective of the scenario is to put the flight maneuver in a practical setting—as the pilot may see it used in a real flight. Instead of simply presenting a turn-around-a-point, the instructor might, for instance, introduce a scenario where the pilot is employed in aerial photography, photographing points on the ground.

In addition to flight maneuvers, a good scenario strives to play up four key components:

1. Situational Awareness—the Big Picture.
2. In Command—the concept of being "in command" is not just a regulatory issue. Being in command must be introduced as the pilot's responsibility for everything associated with the flight and its safe conclusion. A pilot is in command during the planning phase of flight as well as its execution. FITS refers to this as Single Pilot Resource Management.
3. Aeronautical Decision Making—evaluating all information, considering all options and choosing the best one.
4. Managing the risks inherent in every flight.

These are the higher-thinking skills. They allow the pilot to see the accident chain develop before it's too late to recognize the alternatives, and to make the best choice in dealing with his situation.

Limitations of Scenarios

Early in training, the pilot should be told that training will be practical in nature and that training exercises will be as realistic as possible. Mistakes in judgment are expected and are a part of training. The instructor must alert the pilot that he will be expected to handle simulated situations as if he were the sole pilot on board. A pilot will likely be confused and irritated if suddenly thrust into an unexpected, simulated situation and not given the benefit of instructor guidance.

Pilots in general don't like to "fail." When a mistake is made in decision making that affects the flight, it's a much different experience than when altitude was allowed to slide during a maneuver. Learning how to recognize "pilot error" and to manage mistakes is part of the learning process. After the scenario, the instructor leads a debrief so that the pilot discusses with the instructor the problem-solving skills that were used.

Basic knowledge and proficiency in aircraft control is required before introducing a scenario. The pilot should have some understanding of the tasks involved in the scenario. It's difficult to make decisions and to practice being in command if the pilot can't associate the individual tasks. A scenario is a tool best used to "pull it together."

Early scenarios are simple and introduced after basic skills have been achieved. After the pilot has gained more proficiency, then the bar is raised to include more complex situations in higher-thinking skills, completing an effective total training program.

One challenge of a scenario is in keeping the pilot in the mindset of making decisions and in conducting the flight as though the situation were real. If the scenario is conducted on the ground, resist the pilot's recital of "I'd never do that." One way to alleviate "I'd never do that" is to present the situation as if the pilot had been a sleeping passenger who suddenly awoke to find that his pilot-friend put him in this situation. If the scenario is performed in an aviation training device, make it real by engaging in startup and ground maneuvering tasks, just as he would in a real airplane. Make it as real as possible within the limits of the training device.

To be effective, a scenario must be specific to the pilot, the plane and the local flying environment. Specific scenarios that any instructor can use are included in this book. However for maximum benefit, many will need to be revised to relate to the unique needs of the pilot's learning goals.

A Scenario Library

Instructors should have access to a library of scenarios. If the scenario is complex, it will be most effective with a pre-written script to help the instructor manage scenario details. A collection of pre-written and tested scenarios will give the instructor an assortment of tools to use. The library should contain scenarios that offer a range in complexity. Some should feature basic, simple problems. Others should present advanced complex problems to be solved. But the goal of the scenario must be clear and the decision-making opportunities identified to provide a building block approach in developing thinking skills.

Using the scenario library as a "tool box," the instructor can choose from the collection to keep pilots engaged and interested throughout training. Just be sure to choose a scenario appropriate for the pilot's training objectives and skill level.

Conclusions

This chapter introduced scenario concepts, objectives, features and limitations and introduced the instructor's role in joining proficiency in maneuvers with aeronautical decision-making in the certification of pilots. The greater this understanding, the better likelihood that the industry will enjoy increasing numbers of well-trained pilots and safety statistics.

Exercises

1. Think of a time when you imagined different future possibilities to help you solve a problem in your everyday life. For example, a situation at work, with friends or family, or maybe a pet obedience issue. Write a brief summary of:
   - The situation
   - The information you needed
   - The information you wished you could have access to
   - The information you used
   - How you thought about the problem
   - Whether the exercise helped you solve the problem
   - How as a result of finding that solution, you were better equipped to resolve a similar future problem

2. Consider the scenario "Your radios fail. What will you do?"
   - List the implications that the pilot must consider.
   - What situational awareness must the pilot possess?
   - What judgments must be made?
   - What decisions are required by the pilot?
   - What must the pilot do to remain in command of the situation from beginning to end?
   - What underlying concepts must the pilot have knowledge of?
   - How can the instructor help the pilot develop "command mentality"?

Chapter 2

Making a Good Pilot

"If you are looking for perfect safety, you will do well to sit on a fence and watch the birds; but if you really wish to learn, you must mount a machine and become acquainted with its tricks by actual trial."

—*Wilbur Wright, from an address to the Western Society of Engineers (Chicago, September 18, 1901)*

What is a Good Pilot?

What is your definition of a good pilot? The FAA doesn't provide a universal definition of what a *good* pilot is. They define only the minimum requirements in aeronautical knowledge and flight proficiency to pass a practical test.

The aviation industry is therefore free to define itself. It is vital that each instructor define for himself what a *good* pilot is, giving him a goal to aim for and each new pilot an objective worth achieving.

Certainly, a pilot who can control the airplane and exercise good judgment would be included in any definition. Unfortunately, the industry has "extolled judgment as a virtue while ignoring it as a potential training requirement."[1] Scenarios in this book give instructors a variety of practical tools suited to train pilots with judgment. Pilots who are:

- Proficient in precise control of an aircraft
- Able to use cockpit technology to their advantage
- Confident in a wide variety of situations
- Competent in making decisions
- Respectful of flight privileges
- Accountable for their actions
- Safety-minded
- Responsible aviation citizens

While scenario-based training has been proven to be a suitable tool for teaching judgment, proponents don't agree on what a scenario should "contain and what convictions about training it should reflect."[2] The exercises and scenarios in this book maximize:

- Instruction that is efficient and effective
- A learning environment of excellence and being the best
- A safe, fun and organized learning program
- Opportunities for the pilot to experience a variety of situations in a controlled learning program
- Aeronautical decision-making opportunities
- The pilot being "in command" of as many tasks as reasonable, as early as possible
- Learning moments that pull it all together

Teaching judgment and providing decision-making opportunities calls for a syllabus steeped in scenarios that are simple, practical and realistic. Usually, experience is required to develop judgment. But by using scenarios, "expertise can be accelerated and the use of good judgment can be assisted. Pilots perform much better, often in excess of what their experience predicts."[3]

The easiest way to understand how to bring these elements together in making a good pilot is to follow one pilot's training and the scenarios used in his instruction.

Beginning Situational Awareness

Situational awareness is easier to learn and maintain when pilots are directly in control of the aircraft. Flying over the Kentucky River is a perfect place to enjoy an engaging first lesson. The river is just far enough away from the airport for the pilot to be introduced to straight-and-level flight and to experience the effect of the controls before the real fun begins:

> After takeoff on Flight Lesson #1, the pilot is directed towards the river. The river snakes, sometimes in shallow curves, and other times in sharp switchbacks. "Okay, now let's have you fly over the river," the instructor explains. "I'd like you to try to stay exactly over the river. Try to anticipate the turn so that when the river bends sharply you'll turn steeper and when it curves gracefully, you can make a shallow turn." The pilot is focused outside the airplane during the task. He controls the plane and at the same time is aware of the terrain features and obstacles below like the 2,000-foot AGL power plant. When the river meets I-75, the pilot is instructed to follow the road back to the airport. Flying over the interstate seems easy after the previous maneuvering. In addition, the effects of wind become apparent when flying over the straight

highway. The instructor points to the city below and instructs the pilot in how to climb to a higher altitude. Now the pilot is aware of the differences between flying over the congested area versus the rural area of the river. Soon it's time to dial up ATIS and allow the tower to sequence them to the airport. The instructor says, "You're doing such a fine job. Why don't you take charge of flying the airplane while I get our clearance?" The pilot grins and sits tall in the seat.

It's a simple scenario and it's a fun first flight. It allows the pilot to control the flight, not just the airplane, and to understand basic concepts. The lesson doesn't encourage the pilot's head inside the cockpit to maintain headings and altitudes. This lesson allows the pilot to view the big picture: basic aircraft control, attitude flying, looking outside, terrain clearance, traffic avoidance, and safety. And, he learns that during each lesson, he will be expected to handle certain aspects of the flight on his own. This is the basis of situational awareness.

Radio Communications and Beginning Precise Aircraft Control

Radio communications is the easiest of cockpit tasks to be commanded by the pilot. He already knows how to talk. Introduce the radio on Flight Lesson #2. Persuading the pilot to talk on the radio instills great confidence and allows him to consider the world and resources outside the cockpit.

To assist the pilot in communicating, a simple, fill-in-the-blank script is an excellent cockpit tool. The script reminds the pilot of what to say, and to whom. It allows the pilot to take charge of communications while sounding like a Top Gun. See the sample script, "Radio-Call Pilot Aid" in the Appendix (Page 184).

Rehearse the pilot in saying aloud the radio call in the cockpit *before* the mic button is pressed. Other pilots and ATC don't take kindly to nuisance communications. Usually a properly rehearsed and script-equipped pilot will need only encouragement from the instructor to handle normal communications between the ramp area and the runway.

In subsequent flights, expand the pilot's responsibility to include all radio communications when maneuvering on the ground. Later, make the pilot responsible for communications on the ground and in flight, when returning to the airport. As the pilot logs additional flights, prompt the pilot to make communication decisions and to answer the ATC calls of "What are your intentions?" or "What is your request?"

Generally, communications immediately after takeoff are the most demanding for a new pilot and will likely not be assigned until a few additional flights have been logged.

Airborne, each aircraft control maneuver is accomplished with precision. Airspeed, heading, and altitude control are practiced with a sense of excellence and being the best, instead of as a pilot who struggles to stay within the tolerances of the Practical Test Standards. The instructor promotes precision.

As maneuvers are practiced, fly the airplane to its limit. Don't simply teach slow flight, but when the pilot is ready, take the plane to minimum controllable airspeed. Then include turns at minimum controllable airspeed. If flying an airplane capable of spins, don't just discuss spin awareness, but encourage the pilot to learn about spin entries. Allow the pilot to recover from spin entries. Pilots can't learn precise flying until they learn to fly the airplane near its limits and feel confident in their ability to control it.

Beginning Command

Around Flight Lesson #3, the pilot is easing into the routines of preflight inspection, checklists, engine start, taxi and the procedures of getting to the runway hold-short line. This is the time to begin assembling individual tasks into a flight mission and putting the pilot *in command*.

A flight mission is a pre-scripted set of instructions about who, when, where, how and what should be completed. Unlike traditional lesson plans, the flight mission describes not only what maneuvers will be covered but which crewmember (pilot or CFI) will manage which elements. It allows the pilot to take full command of, and responsibility for a subset of flight tasks. The mission assembles individual tasks into the bigger picture, adding to the pilot's situational awareness.

One such flight mission is "Take Me to the Runway." It requires the pilot to handle each of the individual routines associated with getting the airplane ready for flight and for takeoff. A lesson objective might read:

> *Flight Mission:* The instructor will request, "Take me to the runway" allowing the pilot to use the skills and to make the decisions to accomplish this portion of the flight. At this point in training, the pilot is expected to **manage** the preflight inspection, the use of all checklists, engine start, run-up, normal radio communications on the ground, the cockpit technology setup, maneuvering to the runway and calling tower with minimum assistance from the instructor.

The first experience with "Take Me to the Runway" is difficult for both pilot and instructor. This is likely the first lesson to challenge the pilot in assembling his thoughts and making choices on how this portion of the flight will be conducted.

"Take Me to the Runway" challenges the instructor to sit back and be quiet, allotting the pilot the time to sort things out on his own and the freedom to experience his first mistakes—in a controlled environment. After engine start, the pilot will likely begin to fidget and squirm with uncertainty. As a result, the instructor may feel the urge to jump in, to bail the pilot out of his discomfort. *Don't*—pilots should be trained to ask for assistance when it's needed.

Of course, when the pilot requests help, the instructor is there to assist. But a seasoned instructor isn't too quick to jump in and handle every detail. A seasoned instructor provides only the help needed to keep the lesson moving, and then returns "command" back to the pilot. The pilot is given every opportunity to work through the situation on his own before being bombarded with instructor over-helpfulness. The pilot learns that it is sometimes necessary to ask for help—from the instructor, from ATC and from other sources.

The mission must be appropriate to the pilot's level of learning. The individual elements of the mission must include only those individual tasks in which the pilot has demonstrated proficiency. When he's ready, other flight missions could encompass "Take Me to the Practice Area" or "Take Me Home" when returning to the airport after the flight lesson.

As the pilot proceeds further into training, the flight mission should grow to include many more individual tasks. Ultimately before first solo, the pilot is in command of and responsible for the entire flight from preflight planning to tiedown.

Using Cockpit Technology

By about Flight Lesson #4, the pilot is experiencing some unproductive straight-and-level flight time to and from practice areas. Use this time to introduce technology, and specifically, the autopilot if installed.

The autopilot is an excellent start for teaching technology. The autopilot will serve as the foundation upon which introducing additional technology can be built. On a future lesson, the pilot will have the option of allowing the autopilot to control the airplane while, for instance, GPS is being introduced.

Don't overwhelm the new pilot with all the bells and whistles, all at once. At the beginning, introduce the simplest functions. HDG and ALT on the autopilot is a good starting point. After a preflight briefing and an in-flight demonstration of autopilot HDG and ALT functions, the pilot can gain trust in technology to control the plane. After that, the pilot should be put in command of HDG and ALT while returning to the airport.

During subsequent lessons, the basic functions of GPS Direct-To and NRST can be added to fill any otherwise unproductive time. Even if the aircraft is not GPS equipped, a simple hand-held unit will help the pilot develop basic understanding in its concepts.

Go/No-Go Weather

Around four or five flights before solo is a good time for the ground briefing to introduce sources for obtaining a local weather briefing and the elements of the go/no-go decision for a local flight. Positioning the briefing at this point in training provides the pilot with multiple opportunities to make weather decisions under the guidance of the instructor. It allows the pilot to practice preflight planning while under the instructor's direction, prior to solo flights.

After the pilot is assigned responsibility for weather briefings, begin each lesson by allowing the pilot to explain weather conditions and to participate in mission planning. Each flight should set aside five minutes for the instructor and pilot to review reported conditions. If the pilot can't talk about today's weather, it's a sure sign that it's not all together in his head.

Help him relate reported weather to actual conditions. To a new pilot, a METAR is just numbers on the computer screen until the instructor relates it to actual flight conditions. Require the pilot to choose an appropriate altitude for the flight based on reported ceilings and the maneuvers to be practiced. During flight, the instructor can point out actual distance from clouds, estimate actual visibility to a known visual landmark and wind conditions in comparison to the reported conditions. In this way, the pilot learns to associate weather reports to flight conditions.

Then, start the "what if..." game by asking the pilot to consider, "What if the clouds were 500 feet lower, would we be able to maintain a suitable altitude to clear terrain?" "What if the temperature goes down 3 degrees during sunset, how might that affect the base of the clouds?" "What if it goes down 10 degrees?"

The same is true with a TAF. Although the flight lesson will probably not encompass the TAF time period, the instructor can do much to relate the forecast to actual conditions. "You mentioned a cold front?" "Where is that front now?""Which way is it moving?""How fast is it moving?""What time is it expected to move into our area?""What if it arrived one hour sooner, how would that affect our flight?""How about one hour later?"

Now, go fly into the direction of the front. Not away from it—towards it. Fly in the weather. Keep the backdoor open as an escape route home, but allow the pilot to see what the approaching front really looks like, and should trouble begin to brew, where the preferable alternatives might be. The flight mission could look like this:

> *Flight Mission:* The pilot will receive a weather briefing and with the instructor's assistance, make the go/no-go decision. The pilot is expected to **manage** the preflight start, run-up, handle communications, taxi and takeoff with minimum assistance from the instructor. After takeoff, the pilot will remain aware of weather conditions; and after climbing to his chosen altitude, he will **practice** maneuvers en route in the direction of his chosen airport, enter the traffic pattern and **practice** two landings there before returning in the direction of home.

From this Point Forward

At this point, expand the pilot's responsibilities to include preflight planning. The pilot has the skills and thought processes necessary to plan flight missions to include nearby airports. It doesn't have to be a full-blown cross-country and the destination doesn't have to be far away. The idea is only to have a reason to fly, with thought given to the decisions in preflight planning and with maneuvers included as they would be used in a real flight. Plan lessons that include practice sessions en route to a nearby airport where the pilot is expected to enter the traffic pattern for practice in two stop-and-go's before returning to the home airport.

Whenever maneuvers appear in practice sessions, have a practical application for each. Rectangular course is preparation for flights in the traffic pattern. Turns around a point are necessary during aerial photography. Stalls make beautiful landings. Steep turns are used in search-and-rescue missions to facilitate ground resources to the site. Make it fun.

> The Instructor begins, "I have a user-defined waypoint entered into the GPS. I want you to navigate Direct-To REDBARN. You won't have any trouble spotting the Red Barn on the ground. I'd like to take photographs over REDBARN. You get a weather briefing and tell me how we will accomplish this mission…"

During review sessions, divide the time allotted for review into halves. In the first half, as each maneuver is called for, challenge the pilot with one chance—and one chance only—to show pride in his "Best Ability," without assistance. Make it fun, but push him, gently. The second portion of the review time is devoted to polish and refinement. Soon the pilot learns that best ability is expected on each attempt. Best ability shouldn't be something the pilot aspires to only for a checkride. Rather, it becomes his normal, routine flying. However, best ability is just that; perfection is not expected. The instructor must keep the experience positive and keep the pilot's expectations realistic, while continuing to make baby-step improvements.

Beginnings in ADM: The Preflight Risk Checklist

About three flights before solo, a formal introduction to the foundations of risk management should be introduced. While there has been exposure to situational awareness, CFIT and the elements of risk, a formal briefing helps to pull it all together. Some instructors experience problems in teaching risk management in that it is an all-encompassing subject with infinite possibilities. Where to begin? Where to end?

A good start for introducing risks is to confine the first discussion to include only today's flight. Today's flight can best be analyzed for risks with the use of a checklist. A preflight risk checklist is a "structured procedure to assess the level of risk for each flight" (see a sample of this in Table 2-1).[4] The checklist quantifies the major risk elements found in recorded NTSB aviation accidents. Each element is assigned a score. Specific scores are totaled to find an overall risk score for today's flight.

This checklist is an effective instructional tool. It's an uncomplicated way for instructors to introduce and discuss the risk elements in flying. Pilots too, find it helpful to use the checklist in developing judgment. It ensures that risk management is made a part of the preflight planning process. Include the use of the checklist on later flights by referring to it as part of the preflight briefing throughout training.

Even after graduation, the checklist can be valuable to pilots in explaining to passengers why a flight must be postponed. It's especially practical during new aircraft checkouts, when instructors may be encouraging revised personal minimums. It's also effective during flight reviews and instrument proficiency checks to review an important subject with certificated pilots.

The sample checklist can be a template (Table 2-1). Instructors can customize the risk elements associated with the individual flight-training environment and revise the scores as is appropriate for his clientele.

Table 2-1. Preflight Risk Checklist

Pilot error is the most common cause of fatal accidents. Normally, it's not because of one simple mistake, but because of an accumulation of risk elements. Use this checklist before each flight to assist you in evaluating the risk in your flight—it can't promise a perfect flight, but it may help.

Assign an appropriate score (1 to 5) for your flight in the right-hand (Risk Rating) column. Total all entries recorded in the Risk Rating column to obtain a Total Risk Value. Locate the Total Risk Value for this flight at the bottom. Read the notes and enjoy a safe flight.

Name _____Date of Flight _____/_____/_____

	1	2	3	4	5	Risk Rating
Flight Conditions	Day IMC	Day VMC	Night VMC	Night IMC		
Flight Type	IFR	VFR				
Pilot Rating	CFI or ATP	Commercial	PPL with Instrument	PPL w/o IR or Sport Pilot	Solo Student	
Sleep in last 24 hrs	>8 hrs	7–8 hrs		5–6 hrs	Less than 5 hrs	
Flight Visibility	>0 miles	6–9 miles		2–5 miles	Less than 2 miles	
Reported ceiling	>10,000	5,000 – 9,000	3,000 – 4,000	1,000 – 2,000	Less than 1,000 ft	
Crosswind at Departure	0–5 kts	6–10 kts	11–15 kts	16–20 kts	More than 20 kts	
Crosswind at Destination	0–5 kts	6–10 kts no gusts	6–15 kts with gusts	15–20 kts or crosswinds	More than 20 kts, OR major gusts, OR major crosswind	
Weather Stability	Stable		Slow deterioration		Rapid deterioration	
Destination Airport Familiarity	Yes		No			
Hours in aircraft make/model	>200	151–199	50–150	25–50	Less than 25	
Hours in last 90 days	>15	10–15	5–10	3–5	Less than 3	
Last formal, dual recurrent training	>6 mo's	>9 mo's	>12 mo's	>15 mo's	More than 18 mo's	
Total flight hours	>2,500	501–2,000	251–500	100–250	Less than 100	

Record here your Total Risk Value for this Flight >>>>> Students, file in Training Record	
Normal risks. Normal hazards. Use normal flight planning and personal minimums. Stay alert and fly smart.	14 to 30
Riskier than usual. Conduct flight planning with extra care. Consider alternatives to reduce risk of an accident or incident. Review personal minimums and operating procedures.	31 to 40 or a 5 in any row
Conditions present an unacceptable risk factor that must be reduced. Identify areas to modify. Develop contingency plans before takeoff to deal with each high-risk item. Plan alternates and brief passengers on special precautions to be taken during the flight. Consider delaying flight until conditions improve.	>40 or a 5 in any four rows

We value your friendship. Fly safe. Fly smart.

ADM Decision Boxes

Evaluate, discuss and document pilot judgment and decision-making skill with the same diligence as stick and rudder skills. One way to ensure that judgment is made a part of every lesson is by adding it as an element on the lesson plan. A simple "Decision Box" drawn on the lesson plan form provides a place for the instructor to record the decisions made by the pilot during the flight. It provides a reminder to the instructor that it is a part of each debriefing. It demonstrates to the pilot that the importance of thinking-skill is as equally important as the flight skill. (*See the example, "Flight Lesson 4" on Pages 51-52 in Chapter 3.*)

Simple decisions that the pilot should be asked to make may include personal I'M SAFE considerations, weather go/no-go elements, enroute weather, applying reported weather conditions to actual conditions, oil quantity and fuel reserves during preflight, go/no-go preflight inspection discrepancies, runways to use, responses to ATC requests, altitude for today's flight, direction of the flight (which practice area or which local airport), terrain and traffic avoidance, the choice to use technology, etc.

Combining the Weather Briefing and the ADM/Risk Management Briefing lays the groundwork for the pilot's growing competency with making decisions and being in command. Subsequently, if each flight from one through solo includes five minutes with the instructor probing the pilot's decisions, then these skills will be well honed so that after first solo, the pilot is equipped to make safe decisions on subsequent solo flights.

Preparing For Solo

Preparing for a pilot's first solo encompasses much more than mastering the touchdown. By now the pilot is responsible for all preflight planning, cockpit tasks, communications, maneuvers, and decision-making. A lesson objective could look like this:

> *Flight Mission:* You need to fly to Wichita to pick up an alternator for one of the flight school's aircraft. You have the airplane scheduled for tomorrow for your FAA practical test. So, you really need the alternator. You choose which airport in Wichita you want to land at. You obtain a local weather briefing and **perform** the go/no-go evaluation. You **manage** the preflight, start, engine start and run-up, radio communications, taxi and takeoff with minimum assistance from your instructor. **Perform** the traffic pattern entry, **perform** two landings there, and then return in the direction of home. After reaching your chosen altitude, you will **perform** the assigned maneuvers without much assistance from your instructor. Use all available technology to help relieve your cockpit workload. (But some technology may unexpectedly fail!) You will **perform** two

landings at your home airport. You are expected to **manage** any ATC requests, terrain, traffic, and obstacle clearance. As you are preparing for solo, you are expected to handle all flight tasks as the sole pilot on board.

If the instructor is still involved with helping the pilot with the details of a flight and in making the routine decisions, then the pilot is not prepared to handle the tasks in a solo situation. Before solo, the pilot should demonstrate one flight where he acts as the only pilot on board. Only when the pilot demonstrates that the instructor is not needed is the pilot equipped to handle the flight as the solo pilot.

Beginnings in Pilot Judgment:
Judgment Scenario Database

It's time for the instructor to evaluate the pilot's thinking process. Two underlying questions the instructor must answer to himself before allowing the pilot to solo are: (1) "Does the pilot have the correct priorities in mind?" and (2) "Would I be happy with the pilot's decisions if I weren't there to guide him?" It's easy with the right tool.

The Judgment Scenario Database[5] is an Excel worksheet filled with simple ground scenarios. (See Table 2-2, Page 23.) While discussing scenarios together, both pilot and instructor can evaluate the pilot's thinking as he considers each alternative choice and selects his best choice. "Which option would you choose if this scenario happened to you?" is a normal question to be heard during this pre-solo ground briefing.

A word of caution: there are no "right" answers. The "answer" is not the goal. This is not a test. The goal is simply for the pilot to think and to mentally rehearse resolving practical problems—on the ground, so that if the pilot should later find himself in a similar scenario for real, he'd be prepared. The goal for the instructor is to consider the pilot's choice, in that it's justifiable and that the pilot considered the benefits of other options before making a choice.

Instructors can revise scenarios in the Judgment Scenario Database to make them appropriate for the local training environment. Some instructors use a preferred-answer key, but don't show the key to the pilot, it's only for instructor reference and standardization in training.

Review each scenario and given option. Notice the absence of any obvious right or wrong option. Also notice that each option brings new information into the discussion. A smart instructor looks beyond the obvious, bringing in the implications of each option; under what circumstances would one answer be preferred to another and how new alternatives may become obvious as we think carefully through each option.

Pilots may wish for another available option—sometimes it happens in real life, too! Pilots will sometimes remark, "You should have given me…" Nonetheless, carefully think through the available options and choose from the available ones.

There are many considerations in the first scenario. Don't look for the right answer—there isn't one. The learning potential is in considering each of the alternatives on its own merits and once a choice has been made, challenging it. In Kansas, 25 knots of wind may be a normal day, but in a different training environment, the instructor may feel it is a bit much. If the pilot's choice is, let's say, Option C, then when would Option A be the better choice? Would there ever be a time to choose Option D? Giving consideration to each alternative opens the door to discuss technique, technicalities, and regulations. The instructor may reflect on crosswinds, traffic avoidance, being assertive with ATC to get what you feel you need even to the point of declaring an emergency. The implications of a flight to the business airport might include solo restrictions, endorsements, airspace, and navigation to get there, fuel, and…well, the list could go on.

A ground session reviewing portions of the Judgment Scenario Database will give the instructor insights into the decisions that the pilot is likely to make. "The Judgment Scenario Database provides a benchmark in ascertaining pilot judgment and where none has previously been available. If nothing more, it provides a pilot with a tool to develop self awareness and proficiency in ADM"[6] and lead them to further self-study and flight instruction.

With the Judgment Scenario database, instructors have explicit methods to train pilots to detect inadequate decisions before a poor-decision chain gets out of hand. The scenarios go beyond generalizations about error management, providing pilots with specific techniques to use in specific situations.

Continue incorporating the database into preflight and post-flight briefings throughout training. Use it also during pre-solo cross-country ground briefings, pre-checkride ground briefings or anytime the weather forces good pilots to stay grounded. Less is more. One or two scenarios before and after a flight will get the pilot in a thinking frame of mind. Scenarios require time for the pilot to discover for himself the possibilities and to explore his decisions. Instructors should not rush the pilot's thought process.

Table 2-2. Sample from Judgment Scenario Database

Scenario	A	B	C	D
Upon entering the traffic pattern at Regional Airport, winds are reported 280/25 kts. Tower is vectoring traffic to the 8,800-foot Runway 35. You hear a Cherokee ask Tower to use the 5,000-foot Runway 27. The Cherokee is told that Runway 27 is not the active. You decide to:	Accept the clearance to Runway 35 and follow the traffic.	Request Runway 27. But if 27 is not available, continue to Runway 35.	Strongly request Runway 27, be persistent, and inform the tower that crosswinds are unsafe for you to use 35. If 27 is not made available continue to 35.	If 27 is not made available to you at Regional, then divert to Business Airport where the runway is more directly aligned with the wind.
Upon turning base at the uncontrolled field, you see another aircraft on a straight-in final which will conflict with you. You decide to:	Continue. Flash your landing lights to get his attention.	Do a level 360-degree turn for spacing.	Turn right, exit the pattern and re-enter.	Extend your downwind to take spacing behind the straight-in traffic.
You are planning an hour of practice flying in the traffic pattern. To best use your practice time, you decide to:	Challenge yourself with a variety of short field, soft field, slips and go-around at your home airport.	Fly to nearby Small City Airport, where the traffic is less.	Go to an unfamiliar airport.	Go to a challenging airport.
You are practicing solo touch and go's at the controlled field when you become aware of a silent radio. A call to ATC goes unanswered. What will you do?	Squawk 7600. Continue. Watch for light gun signals and comply. If necessary perform a low approach to get the tower's attention and light gun signal.	Depart the traffic pattern and fly to a nearby uncontrolled airport. Land and call the school.	Remain in the traffic pattern. Circle on downwind until seeing light gun signals and comply.	Declare an emergency. Squawk 7600. Land as soon as practical.
You are solo in the traffic pattern when the tower reports winds 260/15G17. You know that the school's maximum wind restriction is 12 kts. What will you do?	Continue. Make the best crosswind landing you can.	Continue. Ask ATC for the runway most aligned with the wind, even if it is not the active.	Divert to another airport with a runway aligned with the wind. Call the school.	Divert to another airport with a longer and wider runway. Call the school.
You are solo in the practice area when you notice the ammeter showing a discharge. What will you do?	Because you have about 2 hours of battery, continue your solo practice before returning to your home airport.	Turn off #2 NAV/COM, lights, auto, return to your home airport, inform ATC of your situation.	Turn off avionics master. Turn off Master Switch to reset overvoltage relay. Determine if the problem is fixed. If indications seem normal, continue with your flight.	Land at the closest airport. Call the school. Prepare for possible radio failure and no-flap landing.
Which statement is true regarding declaring an emergency to ATC?	You must fill out paperwork and appear before the FAA.	You may be asked to fill out paperwork.	You must report the emergency to the NTSB.	You must report the emergency to the school and you may be asked to fill out paperwork.

An interactive, online version of this database is also available at **www.avhf.com**. Here, the participant is able to compare their answers against answers given by 400 general aviation pilots. It's a way for new pilots to compare how often their decisions match those of experienced pilots. There's even a "SHOW ME" button so the participant can step through his decisions, comparing them with those made by others.

For computer-savvy instructors, the program opens the door to what can be done with using PowerPoint or in writing your own online training presentations.

Ready to Solo?

While most instructors are concerned with the pilot's ability to control the airplane on first solo, seasoned pros include the pilot's decision making in the final verdict to solo or not. Specifically, what decisions should a pilot be able to make before first solo? Scenarios should allow the instructor to witness his pilot:

- Demonstrate priorities in aviating, navigating and communicating.
- React properly and promptly to unexpected situations.
- Demonstrate good judgment in go-arounds.
- Demonstrate judgment in wake turbulence avoidance.
- Demonstrate control in normal routines at the local airport.
- Demonstrate consistent stabilized approaches.
- Demonstrate consistent control in approach airspeed throughout final approach to flare.
- Demonstrate power-off, controlled, on centerline, touchdowns in the first 1/3 of runway.
- Understand the full risk of touch and go's versus stop and go's.
- Demonstrate decisions in the Judgment Scenario Database that the instructor is comfortable with.

Table 2-3. Another example from the Judgment Scenario Database

Scenario: You are on short final at uncontrolled, Little City Airport with one other airplane in the pattern when you suddenly recall that you have forgotten to complete the prelanding checklist. You decide to:			
A	**B**	**C**	**D**
Check the flap setting and then land.	Check the mixture and then land.	Keep your head out of the cockpit and land.	Report your go-around to the other traffic and then go-around.

Such a scenario allows the instructor to check the pilot's decisions before solo. The alternatives start a discussion about checklists, communications, right-of-way regulations, traffic avoidance, keeping your head out of the cockpit, as well as the operational aspects of a go-around procedure.

Shorts and Softs

During short-field and soft-field takeoffs and landings is the time to bring out the Pilot's Operating Handbook (POH). The pilot and instructor should calculate the distance needed to take off and land. Locate that distance on the practice runway. For example, by using "the third runway light" or "the second taxiway" the pilot learns to judge runway distance and to control the airplane with precision. Make it fun. Make it a game. Challenge the pilot.

> *Flight Mission:* You have an important job interview in Gage, OK. You have chosen this as the nearest airport because you don't want to chance being late for your interview. As the longer runway is closed for repairs, you must use the smaller runway. It's also covered with a dusting of fresh snow. Before takeoff you and the instructor will refer to the POH to calculate today's takeoff and landing distances for normal, short-field and soft-field conditions. After takeoff you will engage the autopilot and program the GPS direct to Gage Airport. There, you will practice short- and soft-field takeoffs and landings. Departing Gage, at your chosen altitude, you will practice and refine selected maneuvers using your Best Ability. When the instructor asks "take me home," you will program the GPS and engage the autopilot to return to your home airport. You will execute the flight home as if you were the sole pilot on board. Your instructor will be there to assist with decision-making opportunities that come up during the flight.

Achieving performance that is near that which is outlined in the POH gives an added realism to training. Today practice flights can be, for example, 50% more than POH parameters. On a future flight, encourage the pilot to be within 25% more. Practice short-field landings until the stopping point can be accomplished nearly within the published distance, without burning up brakes and tires. Practice soft-field takeoffs until the plane can be rotated near to the distance described. Teach the pilot to trust the performance outlined in the POH.

Night

At night things are the same, only different. The risks for an accident at night are twice what it is during day. Include early morning sunrise night lessons as well as night after sunset. Night flying brings its own set of unique flight situations for the pilot to be aware of. Consider another example from the Judgment Scenario Database (Table 2-4).

Table 2-4

Scenario: On a VFR night flight, the weather is clear with widely scattered, isolated thunderstorms. You are on a 1-mile final to Regional Airport when a lightning strike from an approaching thunderstorm hits the ground control box, disabling the airport lights. The beacon, runway, taxiway lights are all inop. However, the area is illuminated from FBO, ramp and terminal lights. You decide to:			
A	**B**	**C**	**D**
Land. Get on the ground as soon as possible and out of the path of the approaching thunderstorm.	Go around. Re-enter the traffic pattern and evaluate the situation from traffic pattern altitude.	Go around. Depart the area. Land at Small City Airport, 10 miles south.	Go around. Circle the area outside of the thunderstorm until it passes, then land at Regional once the storm clears the airport.

Cross-Country

At an airport so equipped, request a light gun demonstration from ATC. This allows the pilot to see actual light gun signals. On a possible future fight—when the situation is stressful—he'll know where and what to look for.

Cross-country is another time to pull out the POH. During cross-country planning, have the pilot determine aircraft fuel burn, true airspeed and endurance by researching and interpolating exact performance from the POH. Top off the fuel before departure, if weight and balance allows, even if full fuel is not required. At cross-country destinations, plan to stop and top off again so that the pilot can see the actual fuel burned on that leg.

The cross-country scenario is not complete until the pilot is able to achieve the aircraft performance near to that published in the POH. Navigation, locating a new airport, and entering a strange traffic pattern are not large tasks to conquer at this point—he's already had the experience of flying to new and different airports if earlier scenarios were used properly. The cross-country scenario includes developing trust in the POH. The POH is accurate, but only when the pilot understands when his fuel tanks are *really full*, how to climb precisely, trim properly, fly coordinated, track time accurately and lean carefully.

Cross-country flights that return home along the same route flown out on lend little new learning opportunities. Plan cross-countries to be at least a triangle. There is no need to add realism to cross-country lessons; however with longer flight time, come more opportunities for pilot decision making and learning opportunities.

> *Flight Mission:* You have business meetings in two different cities. Your company is looking to purchase an airplane and you have arranged the two best candidates for your boss to inspect. You will plan and conduct a dual cross-country flight along a triangular route. You will choose one leg to fully use all available technology. One leg will use no technology, controlling the plane without assistance of autopilot and practicing dead reckoning and pilotage. The last leg may or may not use technology, as practice necessitates. You will choose a different form of navigation, (GPS, VOR, and pilotage) for each leg, giving you additional practice in all navigation types. You will choose each takeoff and each landing, practicing short- and soft-field takeoffs and landings. Perhaps a simulated flap failure could precipitate the need for a slip. You will choose the altitude: on one leg to fly as low as is safe, on one leg to fly as high as practical, and on the last leg based on the most favorable winds. Your boss will travel with you or, in the event he is too busy, another person he's designated to fly with you on this flight. You are to **perform** weight and balance, fuel loadings and passenger needs. At each cross-country destination, you will stop and estimate actual fuel used. You will fuel your own aircraft. Your estimate should be within 2 gallons of the actual fuel used.

Adding a passenger on dual cross-countries puts weight and balance into better perspective and gives the pilot another person apart from himself to be responsible for. The aircraft controls feel a little different with weight in the back seat, and takeoffs and landings require more runway. All in all, it adds practice and realism to how the pilot will probably be flying after graduation.

The additional passenger could be another student-pilot. By training two pilots simultaneously, the instructor can afford a longer flight away from home with one pilot flying, followed by the flight back (along a different route) with the other pilot flying. Both pilots fly farther, seeing new terrain and different airspace without being burdened with the additional cost for a longer lesson.

Table 2-5. Another example from the Judgment Scenario Database.

Scenario: You are planning a night cross-country to grandma's. Winds and weather favor cruising at 10,500 MSL. The tailwinds forecast will enable you to make your destination with a 60-minute fuel reserve in one hop. You decide to:			
A	**B**	**C**	**D**
Let down early and cruise the last 30 minutes at a much lower altitude if fuel permits.	Stay up at altitude as long as possible before performing an enroute descent.	Make sure there is a working oxygen system on board in case you need it.	Plan to use oxygen for this flight.

Even in the cross-country phase of training, Judgment Scenarios allow the instructor to introduce rationale for real flights that the pilot may make in the future. This scenario opens the door to discuss family pressures associated with a trip to grandma's, trusting forecasted tailwinds, night flights at 10,500 MSL, smart fuel reserves, supplemental oxygen regulations, the physiological considerations of letting down early versus the operational considerations of staying high as long as possible and statistics that point to fuel exhaustion accidents in trying to make such a trip in "one hop." You weren't looking for the right answer, were you?

The Diversion

As cross-country training begins, training in the diversion-to-an-alternate soon follows. The diversion is difficult to teach in the airplane but is one of the most important tasks a pilot will learn. Done correctly it is the single skill proven to save lives. Pilots, by their nature, find themselves flying over unfamiliar terrain and into unfamiliar airspace. Consider too that the pilot may have traveled from out of state to attend your flight school. When he returns to his local area to fly, he is suddenly flying over terrain that's different from where the training occurred.

The diversion can be especially problematic when depending on a GPS direct-to. Many pilots have found themselves entering special use airspace while circumnavigating weather. Some have found themselves on the sides of mountains. This diversion exercise will highlight the priorities and allow your pilot to make decisions faster.

The diversion is an exercise in decision making but it also stresses the importance of processing all pertinent facts:

- What information do I need to know?
- What additional information will I wish I have?
- How will I have this information available in the cockpit during future flights?

This exercise requires a sectional, a plotted course and an X, indicating the pilot's current position. The exercise begins with the instructor introducing a realistic need for a diversion. The pilot is equipped with airport data on three possible airport alternatives shown in the tables to the right of each scenario exercise. The pilot must choose one. Only that information which would routinely be available in the cockpit is given, such as AFD or GPS database airport info.

The instructor uses a stopwatch to time the exercise and the pilot's decision. The time-critical factor adds realism and a little extra tension. During any decision-making exercise, if the available time is limited, the ability to properly evaluate all alternatives is stressful and the outcome is often poor. Chances for making the right decision depend on the pilot's ability to evaluate all pertinent information, quickly.

Diversion exercise scenarios begin on the next page (chapter text resumes on Page 38).

Diversion Exercise Scenario #1

The first scenario begins with the pilot in his local area, airspace and terrain. The following is an example of one.

You are flying at 4,500 MSL on a flight westbound from Charleston, West Virginia to Lexington, Kentucky in a Cessna 172 (TAS 110 knots) when you realize that weather conditions are deteriorating below the requirements for visual meteorological conditions. You decide to land.

The time now is 1700 local and you have a fuel endurance of 60 minutes remaining. Your task is to determine, as quickly and as accurately as possible, which of the alternates is most appropriate under the circumstances. Which airport will you choose?

Note: Instructor will time your response.

1. Flemington-Mason
2. Mount Sterling
3. Morehead

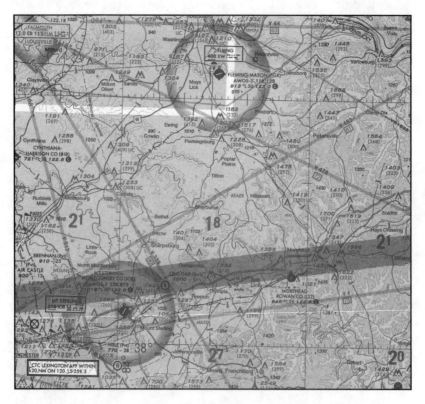

For a close-up version of this sectional excerpt, see Page 185 in the Appendix.

Table 2-6. Airport alternatives for Scenario #1

Scenario #1	Option 1 Fleming-Mason	Option 2 Mount Sterling	Option 3 Morehead
Distance	16 NM	25 NM	11 NM
Heading	330 degrees	232 degrees	185 degrees
Elevation	913 feet	1,019 feet	845 feet
Runways	07/25	03/21	05/23
Runway condition	Good	Fair	Poor
Runway length	5,001 × 75 feet	5,002 × 75 feet	2,600 × 75 feet
Runway type	Asphalt	Asphalt	Asphalt
Displaced threshold	40 feet	Nil	Nil
Runway lights	Yes (pilot operated)	Yes (pilot operated)	No
Navaids	NDB	NDB	None
Landing fee	None	$10	None
Control tower	None	None	None
Location	7 NM N of Flemingsburg	2 NM W of Mount Sterling	6 NM SW of Morehead
Fuel facilities	Yes	No	Yes
Maintenance	No	No	No
Accommodations	None on site	None on site	None on site
METAR	KFGX CURRENT 09003KT 3 RSH OVC020 16/15	KIOB CURRENT 13010KT 3BR OVC020 15/14	I32 CURRENT 17015KT 3DZ OVC010 16/15
Lowest safe altitude	1,996 feet	1,904 feet	1,785 feet
End of daylight	1753 local	1753 local	1751 local

Diversion Exercise Scenario #2

The second scenario removes the pilot from his local area and places him in unknown terrain.

You are westbound at 10,500 MSL from Yakima, Washington to Portland, Oregon in a Cessna 172 (TAS 110 knots) when you realize that snow showers have deteriorated visibility to near white-out conditions. You decide to land.

It is currently 1735 local time and you have a fuel endurance of 60 minutes. Your task is to determine, as quickly and as accurately as possible, which of the alternates is most appropriate under the circumstances. You have three options available as alternates. Which will you choose?

Note: Instructor will time your response.

1. Columbia Gorge
2. Hood River
3. Cascade Locks State

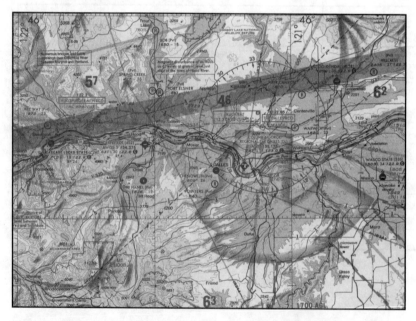

For a close-up version of this sectional excerpt, see Page 186 in the Appendix.

Table 2-7. Airport alternatives for Scenerio #2

Scenario #2	Option 1 Columbia Gorge	Option 2 Hood River	Option 3 Cascade Locks State
Distance	32 NM	27 NM	31 NM
Heading	155 degrees	183 degrees	213 degrees
Elevation	247 feet	151 feet	845 feet
Runways	13/20	06/24	05/23
Runway conditions	Good	Fair	Poor
Runway dimensions	5,097 × 150 feet	3,040 × 75 feet	1,800 × 30 feet
Runway type	Asphalt	Asphalt	Asphalt
Displaced threshold	200 feet	Nil	Nil
Runway lights	Yes (pilot operated)	No	No
Navaids	VOR 7 NE	None	None
Landing fee	None	$20	None
Control tower	None	None	None
Location	2 NM NE of The Dalles	2 NM S of Hood River	6 NM SW of Morehead
Refuelling facilities	Yes	No	Yes
Maintenance facilities	Yes	No	No
Accommodations	None on site	None on site	None on site
METAR	KDLS CURRENT 23007KT 3 DZ OVC020 12/11	IS2 CURRENT 25009KT 3 BR OVC015 15/14	KCZK CURRENT 27010KT 3 SH OVC015 14/12
Lowest safe altitude	4,600 feet	5,700 feet	5,700 feet
End of daylight	1753 local	1751 local	1753 local

Diversion Exercise Scenario #3

You are undertaking a flight, northeast, from Fort Collins, Colorado to Searle, Nebraska in a Cessna 172 (TAS 110 knots) when you realize that the ceiling has deteriorated below the requirements for visual meteorological conditions.

It is currently 1735 local time. You have been forced to descend lower and lower and are currently having difficulty maintaining 7,100 MSL. You have a fuel endurance of 60 minutes. Your task is to determine, as quickly and as accurately as possible, which of the alternates is most appropriate under the circumstances. You have three options available as alternates. Which will you choose?

Note: Instructor will time your response.

1. Kimball
2. Sidney
3. Sterling

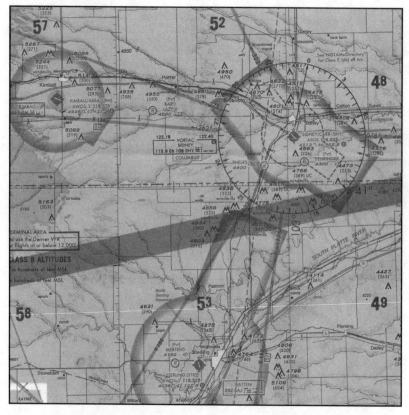

For a close-up version of this sectional excerpt, see Page 187 in the Appendix.

Table 2-8. Airport alternatives for Scenario #3

Scenario #3	Option 1 Kimball	Option 2 Sidney	Option 3 Sterling
Distance	28 NM	41 NM	23 NM
Heading	006 degrees	057 degrees	107 degrees
Elevation	4,926 feet	4,313 feet	4,038 feet
Runways	10/28	12/39	15/33
Runway condition	Good	Fair	Good
Runway dimensions	6,199 × 75 feet	6,600 × 100 feet	4,730 × 75 feet
Runway type	Concrete	Concrete	Asphalt
Displaced threshold	None	40 feet	200 feet
Runway lights	Yes (pilot operated)	Yes (pilot operated)	Yes (pilot operated)
Navaids	NDB	VOR	NDB 5 SE
CTAF frequency	Yes	No	123.0
Landing fee	None	None	Yes
Control tower	None	None	None
Location	3 NM S of Kimball	3 NM S of Sidney	3 NM W of Sterling
Refuelling facilities	No	Yes	Yes
Maintenance facilities	None on site	None on site	Yes
Accommodations	None on site	None on site	None on site
METAR	KIBM CURRENT 15015KT 2 SN OVC023 13/12	KSNY CURRENT 16010KT 2 BL SN OVC025 15/14	KSTK CURRENT 17012KT 2 SN OVC024 13/12
Lowest safe altitude	5,800 feet	5,300 feet	5,800 feet
End of daylight	1753 local	1751 local	1753 local

Diversion Exercise Scenario #4

You are undertaking a northeast flight from La Junta, Colorado to Hays, Kansas at 7,500 MSL in a Cessna 172 (TAS 110 knots) when you realize that headwinds coupled with moderate/severe turbulence are becoming unbearable. You decide to land.

It is currently 1735 local time and you have a fuel endurance of 60 minutes. Your task is to determine, as quickly and as accurately as possible, which of the alternates is most appropriate under the circumstances. You have three options available as alternates. Which will you choose?

Note: Instructor will time your response.

1. Oakley
2. Dighton
3. Trego Wakeeney

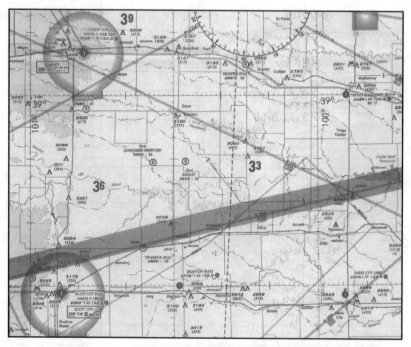

For a close-up version of this sectional excerpt, see Page 188 in the Appendix.

Table 2-9. Airport alternatives for Scenario #4

Scenario #4	Option 1 Oakley	Option 2 Dighton	Option 3 Trego Wakeeney
Distance	27 NM	21 NM	24 NM
Heading	312 degrees	195 degrees	063 degrees
Elevation	3,045 feet	2,778 feet	2,435 feet
Runways	16/34	17/35	17/35
Runway conditions	Fair	Good	Fair
Runway length	5,000 × 75 feet	2,400 × 40 feet	4,000 × 50 feet
Runway type	Asphalt	Asphalt	Asphalt
Displaced threshold	None	30 feet	20 feet
Runway lights	Yes (pilot operated)	Yes (pilot operated)	Yes (pilot operated)
Navaids	NDB	None	None
Control tower	None	No	No
Location	2 NM SE of Oakley	1 NM NW of Dighton	2 NM SW of Wakeeney
Refuelling facilities	Yes	No	Yes
Maintenance facilities	No	No	No
Accommodations	None on site	None on site	None on site
METAR	KOEL CURRENT 22005KT 3 DS CLR 13/09	K65 CURRENT 22008KT 3 DS CLR 13/08	OHI CURRENT 22510KT 3 DU CLR 13/09
Lowest safe altitude	3,600 feet	3,600 feet	3,300 feet
End of daylight	1753 local	1751 local	1753 local

Generally, a set of four scenarios is appropriate to teach the diversion concepts. The first scenario should include a flight segment on the local sectional and near the home airport. The next scenario should place the pilot in an unknown geography and terrain. The scenario that follows should add airspace to the challenge. The last scenario should present difficult options.

The instructor should NOT quickly offer "I think the right answer is…" Rather, he should help the pilot discover his own preferred answer through reasoning. Expect the pilot to make his choice based on his experience rather than that of the instructor's. Expect the pilot to use 15 minutes or more to make an informed choice on the first scenario. It's a scenario; there is no right or wrong answer. The instructor must only assure that the pilot considered all pertinent information and evaluated all available options to make a choice that can be justified by real data given the priorities. The second scenario normally requires about half the time to make a choice and even with new situations being introduced in subsequent scenarios, information is correlated for a faster response time.

With the advent of glass cockpits, this scenario may seem obsolete. It's not, but the scenario does need to be adapted for TAA technology: avionics screen shots take the place of an Airport Facility Directory. Until manufacturers provide a way to save actual screen shots, a digital camera is the best tool. Take photos of the MFD terrain/weather/airspace plus photos of pertinent Airport Data screens.

The scenarios are timed, yet a speedy decision is not the ultimate goal. The real lesson is that the pilot learns what to assess, what information is pertinent and how to process all available information to make an informed best choice. The objective of the scenario is for the pilot to consider each option on its merits, concluding in a safe landing. The instructor must ensure that the pilot considers *all available information*.

Preparing for Graduation

During later lessons, the flight is again divided into halves with the first half assuming the pilot's "Best Ability" without prompting or assistance. Polish and refinement are given on the second half. It should be evident that best ability is expected on each attempt. It should be apparent at this point in training that best ability has been instilled as the pilot's routine, rather than something he aspires to on-demand or for a checkride.

Seasoned instructors have long used the "Perfect Flight" as the final test prior to graduation. During the Perfect Flight, the pilot gets one chance—and one chance only—to perform the entire flight without assistance. This does not imply that a pilot is expected to perform with perfection. It does mean that he is expected to:

1. Apply aeronautical knowledge to solve problems and make decisions.
2. Work towards consistent precision, controlling the airplane *and* the situation.
3. Take action based on the best choice among all available options.
4. Prioritize tasks and deal with the unexpected.
5. Command technology and solicit sources outside the cockpit at his leisure.
6. Recognize when things don't "seem right" and take steps for further research.

This lesson done correctly requires the instructor to do absolutely nothing, unless an unsafe situation requires his action. It requires the pilot to be the one "in command" and to control the flight as if he were the sole pilot on board. Let's say the instructor calls for a stall. The pilot is expected at this point in training to recognize that his altitude is too low without soliciting the instructor's input and to take corrective climb before beginning the maneuver. Let's say the instructor calls for a Direct-To, the pilot is expected to recognize an airspace incursion and take corrective action without the instructor drawing attention to it.

After the Checkride: Personal Minimums

After the checkride, there remains one additional ground lesson for the instructor to complete with the new pilot: a discussion of suggested personal minimums. Consider another example from the Judgment Scenario Database:

Table 2-10

Scenerio: You're flying a CFI from your old flight school to Nearby Airport to pick up an airplane "returned to service." Both you and your CFI arrive at the airport later than planned and feel rushed. He offers to help with the preflight. You decide to:			
A	**B**	**C**	**D**
It's your plane; you take care of getting the flight ready to go.	Have him get the weather, NOTAMs, and file the flight plan while you preflight the airplane.	Have him preflight the airplane while you get the weather, NOTAMs, and file.	Ask him who should do what.

This scenario is a lead-in to personal minimums. Personal minimums encompass not only weather minimums, but all standard operating procedures that the new pilot will be using long after he's graduated from under the watchful eye of his diligent instructor. Who hasn't at some point in a flying career found themselves in just such a situation? It points up the legalities of being pilot-in-command, but also the situation of two pilots flying together, especially when the more experienced pilot is not the pilot-in-command. At what point will your pilot defer his command to another pilot on the basis of ratings or hours? At what point will your pilot trust the judgments and decisions of another pilot?

Now reverse the roles. If your pilot is riding along with a seemingly more experienced pilot, what information should your pilot gather about the other pilot? What are the implications of the new pilot flying along with an aircraft owner in his airplane? How should one pilot evaluate another pilot before climbing in and going for a ride? These mental rehearsals may prove to be very important in the pilot's future.

Thoughts about Regulations

The preferred technique for teaching Federal Aviation Regulations is to cover the regulations that support the scenario. Regulations should not be a stand-alone ground lesson. Nor should regulations be taught as a separate subject—to do so encourages rote memorization but not understanding or application. Regulations should be introduced as a part of the total flight scenario so that the pilot learns the practical application of the regulation.

For example, during a weather briefing would be the perfect time to discuss the regulations pertaining to cloud clearances and visibility, preflight action, and other weather regulations that support the go/no-go decision. During a night flight is the time to introduce night regulations. And during a dual flight with an approved passenger is the time to speak of passenger-carrying regulations.

Homework and Note-Taking

Interesting and engaging homework is required to remember information learned from the scenario. A criticism of aviation instructors is that "aeronautical knowledge is taught in the abstract, that is to say, outside of the context in which they are to be used."[7]

Scenario-based training helps to bring abstract concepts into context. Many instructors use mnemonics to help pilots remember aeronautical knowledge. This only helps to select the right option on a test question, but does not help them remember how to use the material. Six months after certification, graduates routinely forget significant material tested by the FAA knowledge questions. In fact, routine flying and recency requirements does not replace the need for ongoing self-study.

Rather than teach a mnemonic, put it to use in a real flight scenario. Get the pilot involved in interactive learning and Internet research. Regular assignments for self-study and homework allow the pilot to be engaged in learning when not at the airport.

A notebook can be a pilot's best tool. Encourage the pilot to keep a pilot journal. For those periods when training is interrupted, a pilot journal can engage them mentally even when not at the airport. It helps to keep questions organized for review with the instructor during the next training session. A simple spiral bound notebook is all that is necessary to help a pilot to organize homework, thoughts and questions about flying.

Conclusions

The pilot trained in the course outlined in this chapter started ahead of the pack by having goals for graduation clearly defined—not against minimum standards, but within standards adopted by industry as those being representative of an aviation citizen.

Most pilots, and instructors, mistakenly believe that good judgment is only acquired through years of flying experience. However, new pilots of little experience cannot rely on experience as a teacher. "Generally speaking, pilots do not normally make important decisions based on a single factor alone."[8]

A course of training steeped in exercises that promote situational awareness and risk management gives pilots a head start on thinking and making decisions. A course that promotes the pilot as being "in command" in the early stages of training gives the pilot practice in carrying out the decisions made and practice in "mistake management" while under the guidance of the instructor.

The pilot was given responsibility early on and placed "in command," first of radio communications and preflight inspection. Then his individual responsibilities were melded together. Flight missions such as "take me home" introduced him to the safety system—as a pilot, flying an airplane, over terrain, in a national airspace, and perhaps controlled by ATC. He learned how to use and control system elements to his advantage.

A judgment made and tested in the training environment builds confidence. The Judgment Scenario Database provided the benchmark in ascertaining the pilot's judgment.

Finally, a lot of homework and self-study was required after the scenario to help the pilot to remember and reflect on what had been learned. A pilot trained in a course such as the one just outlined is a very mature pilot in the sense that his expertise far exceeds his total flight hours.

Exercises

1. What is *your* definition of a good pilot?

2. This Chapter refers to a responsible "aviation citizen." What would be *your* definition of an aviation citizen?

3. Write a fun and engaging first lesson scenario for your local area.

4. Go to **www.asf.org** and complete one of the free online courses found there. Would such a course be an effective homework or self-study assignment that an instructor could assign to his pilot?

5. Consider the examples given in this chapter, and then write a set of diversion scenarios using current navigation charts. Keys for successful diversion scenarios include:

  • Give the pilot the big picture with a realistic mission, departure and destination, even though the diversion will concentrate on one small section of the route.

  • Move subsequent scenarios outside familiar area, airspace and terrain.

  • Give the pilot enough of the chart so that he has the big picture.

  • Don't provide one clearly "correct" choice.

  • Stress the need to evaluate all available information.

  • Ask the pilot to justify his answer based on real information.

  • Bring to light any pertinent information that you feel was overlooked.

6. Describe a situation when you would not accept a ride with a more experienced pilot in a cool airplane you've always dreamed of flying.

Chapter 3

Syllabus Redesign

Organizing the Lesson

The job of any syllabus is to organize learning tasks. But knowing something versus knowing when to use that knowledge are two separate skills. In addition to learning information, the pilot must learn to apply the information in routine flights; thus "mastery of the information and its implications is required." [1]

Incorporate Scenarios

One purpose of including scenarios within a training syllabus is to practice applying routine information to tasks in new and different settings. The exposure to familiar tasks in new and changing settings closely resembles real-life flying. With practice, the pilot's application of the information is improved and his judgment in choosing appropriate information is improved. Judgment is "like intelligence; its impact is recognized in behavior, but a precise definition remains elusive." [2]

Scenario-based training today is closely linked to FITS. Instructors who fully embrace the concepts of scenario-based training may wish to author a syllabus specifically having scenarios as its core. Such is the case with a FITS syllabus. However, writing a complete syllabus from scratch requires much time and effort. Another option is to use a familiar, generic, commercially available syllabus and redesign it to include scenarios and other FITS philosophies.

This chapter compares FITS training to traditional flight training methods. It presents a sample FITS lesson plan compared to a commercially available lesson plan that has been redesigned to include FITS concepts. Included are hints for authoring a FITS-accepted syllabus and points to help an instructor in redesigning a syllabus.

Understanding FAA/Industry Training Standards (FITS)

The FAA is unable to regulate safety in pace with "current and future operational problems." With FITS, the FAA partners with industry; with flight instructors, aircraft manufacturers and training providers to affect voluntary, flight training improvements.

FITS expects to increase safety by reducing accidents caused by human factors. To accomplish this task, training is moved away from traditional maneuvers and more into thinking skills. With the help of scenario-based training, pilots are taught to consider the risks of flying and how to choose the most appropriate way to deal with the risks. "But FITS is not an ad hoc module to be discussed only at the end of an instructional program. Instead, FITS principles are integrated throughout the training process."

FITS vs. Traditional Training:
A Comparison Revised by Author

In the traditional flight lesson, an instructor might explain, for instance, how to perform a turn around a point. The preflight briefing centers on how to perform the maneuver. The pilot would learn about wind corrections; the difference between aircraft heading and course; airspeed versus groundspeed. The instructor would demonstrate the ground reference maneuver, and with repeated practice, the pilot would learn to perform the maneuver within acceptable tolerances.

In a FITS lesson, the pilot might be asked to plan a flight to a nearby airport. There is a reason to fly; for instance, the pilot has been hired to take photos of the Big Red Barn. The preflight briefing includes not only the specifics of the maneuver, but also how the skills are used in real life. After reaching an acceptable standard, the pilot then puts it to practical application. But more, the pilot is also asked to think and consider airport information and communications, runways, and alternate courses of action in preparation for unexpected situations. Upon arrival at the destination, the pilot chooses (with minimum guidance from the instructor) how to enter and fly the traffic pattern using the proper wind drift strategies. In the end, the pilot understands the practical application of the maneuver in the real world and is capable of *explaining* the varied cockpit tasks with emphasis; not on the maneuver, but on situational awareness, CFIT and controlling the airplane in a variety of wind conditions.

In the traditional lesson, the pilot is focused on the maneuver rather than the Big Picture—the "combination of people, procedures, equipment, facilities, software, tools, and materials needed to perform a specific task." The FITS lesson compels the pilot to consider the maneuver as one element in the Big Picture. The goal is to increase the pilot's competence in controlling all aspects of the flight. By teaching the pilot to think, the instructor teaches the skills to be used in handling new "combinations of circumstances not contemplated" and not specifically practiced during training. FITS refers to the Big Picture as "system safety."

Writing a FITS Syllabus

A FITS syllabus looks completely different from a traditional one (see example later in this chapter). The FITS syllabus is specific to the training environment, the equipment installed in the training aircraft and the local cross-country flights available for scenario constructs. Thus it would be difficult for professional syllabus writers to offer a generic, one size for all, FITS syllabus.

A FITS lesson plan uses a "structured script of real world scenarios to address flight training objectives in the operational environment."

- Every FITS flight lesson, beginning with the first, is conducted as a scenario, usually a cross-country.
- Each phase of flight—preflight, taxi, etc., includes an aspect of pilot decision-making and risk management.
- In the appropriate phases of flight, each FITS lesson includes situational awareness and single-pilot resource management. It assumes that as training progresses, the pilot is in command and will demonstrate single-pilot resource management.

The FAA website offers guidance materials for anyone to use in authoring a syllabus intended for FITS acceptance. There, an instructor can find a combined private/instrument FITS syllabus used by Middle Tennessee State University that can be downloaded and customized. (See Figure 3-1 on the next page.)

Once the new FITS syllabus is complete, the local FSDO office has responsibility for reviewing and accepting the syllabus on behalf of a National FITS Committee. After the FSDO determines that the syllabus fully employs FITS philosophies, instructors are permitted to include the FITS logo in advertising "FITS Accepted" materials.

The key to success in obtaining FITS acceptance in writing the syllabus grounded in scenario-based training, single-pilot resource management and learner-centered grading. (Learner-centered grading is covered in Chapter 4.)

Single-pilot resource management is included throughout a FITS training scenario. In days gone-by, pilots talked of being "in command." The term described the many roles of the pilot other than manipulat-

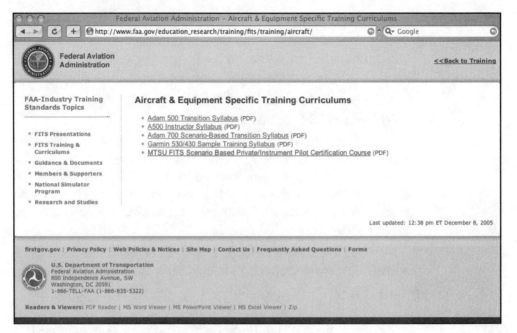

Figure 3-1. MTSU FITS syllabus webpage.

ing the controls. Today, FITS applies "in command" equally to single-pilot resource management. Specifically, single-pilot resource management includes:

- Situational Awareness
- Positive Aircraft Control
- Risk Management
- Aeronautical Decision Making
- Automation/Tasks Management
- Controlled Flight Into Terrain Awareness

Redesigning a Commercially-Available Syllabus

Redesigning a familiar, generic syllabus requires the instructor to fill every minute with teaching opportunities. Using the listed maneuvers as the core of the lesson, the instructor practices maneuvers within a scenario, incorporates installed cockpit technology and provides opportunities for pilot decision-making and single-pilot resource management.

As an example, the Flight Lesson #4 Lesson Plan shown later in the chapter is not a cross-country scenario as would be expected in the FITS syllabus. Rather, it is a lesson that incorporates maneuvers training into the format of a flight from point A to B. The aspiring pilot is expected to manage a small portion of the flight. On subsequent lessons, the pilot would be expected to take on additional responsibilities and command more of the flight. Along the way, the instructor finds opportunities to incorporate the concepts of risk management, automation, and controlled flight into terrain awareness. The instructor seeks out ways to develop the pilot's situational awareness. An example of how to include these concepts was covered in Chapter 2.

The preflight discussion must include a briefing on the thinking skills used in this lesson. Use ground scenarios, similar to the Judgment Scenario Database, in the preflight briefing.

If the training aircraft is equipped with technology—that is, at least an autopilot and GPS—then lessons should include an avionics component. Don't overwhelm the pilot with everything all at once, but introduce functions that support the scenario.

After the pilot demonstrates proficiency in the task, then make the pilot responsible for that task. The pilot is expected to **perform** and **manage** the task whenever it is needed on future flights without prompting and with minimum assistance from the instructor.

Include a Decision Box. Pilot judgment should be evaluated and recorded as flight skills. Only by discussing and analyzing the decisions can this portion of training be considered of equal importance. If lesson after lesson the Decision Box is void, it may indicate to the instructor that not enough opportunities are being made available for the pilot to practice decision skills.

Sample FITS Lesson Plan

Table 3-1

Phase of Flight	Scenario Activities	Desired Scenario Outcome
Flight Planning	1. Scenario Planning	1. Practice
	2. Weight and Balance and Aircraft Performance Calculations	2. Practice
	3. Preflight, Single Pilot Resource Management Briefing	3. Practice
	4. Decision Making and Risk Management	4. Practice
Normal Preflight and Cockpit Procedures	1. Normal Pre-Takeoff Checklist Procedures	1. Manage
	2. GPS Programming	2. Practice
	3. MFD & PFD Setup	3. Practice
Engine Start and Taxi Procedures	1. Engine Start	1. Manage
	2. Taxi	2. Manage
	3. Single Pilot Resource Management & Situational Awareness	3. Practice

Continued on next page...

Slow Flight and Stalls	1. Slow Flight	1. Perform
	2. Recovery from Power On and Power Off Stalls	2. Perform
	3. Aeronautical Decision Making and Situational Awareness	3. Practice
GPS Operation and Programming	1. Direct-To	1. Practice
	2. Airport Information and Approach Select	2. Practice
	3. Flight Plan	3. Practice
Autopilot Programming	1. Altitude Hold	1. Practice
	2. Navigation and Auto Trim Modes	2. Practice
	3. Flight Director/PFD Interface	3. Explain
Avionics Interface	1. Identification of Data/Power Sources	1. Explain
	2. Identification of PFD Failure Modes	2. Explain
	3. Aircraft Automation Management	3. Explain
Data link Situational Awareness Systems and Additional Avionics Setup	1. Data Link Weather Setup and Operation	1. Practice
	2. Data Link Traffic Setup and Operation	2. Practice
	3. Data Link Terrain Display and Warning Setup and Operation	3. Practice
	4. Data link Flight Planning and Traffic Control Setup and Ops	4. Practice
Emergency Procedures	1. Backup—Instrument Unusual Attitude Recovery	1. Practice
	2. Autopilot Unusual Attitude Recovery	2. Practice
	3. Engine failure/Emergency Descent	3. Practice
	4. Risk Management and Decision Making	4. Practice
Descent	1. VNAV Planning	1. Practice
	2. Navigation Programming	2. Practice
	3. Manual and Autopilot Descent	3. Practice
	4. Situational Awareness, CFIT Avoidance	4. Practice
Instrument Approach Procedure	1. Manual and Coupled ILS	1. Practice
	2. Manual and Autopilot Assisted Missed Approach	2. Practice
	3. Procedure Turn	3. Manage
	4. Task Management and Decision Making	4. Decide
Landing	1. Before Landing Procedures	1. Manage
	2. IFR Landing Transition	2. Practice
	3. Normal Landing	3. Manage
	4. Go-Around	4. Decide
	5. Aeronautical Decision Making and Situational Awareness	5. Practice
Aircraft Shutdown and Securing Procedure	1. Aircraft Shutdown and Securing Checklist	1. Manage
	2. Aircraft Towing, Ground Handling, and Tie Down	2. Manage

Sample of a Commercially-Available Syllabus (plus FITS)

See Table 3-2 on the next page.

Flight Lesson 4 "Take Me to the Runway" DUAL LOCAL

Mission: You are flying to Louisville to pick up your daughter and deliver her home for the holidays. The instructor will request "Take me to the runway" allowing you to use the skills and make the decisions to accomplish that portion of the flight. At this point in training, you are expected to **manage** the preflight inspection, checklists, engine start, run up, normal radio communications on the ground, cockpit technology setup, and maneuver to the runway; ready to call tower with minimum help from the instructor. During flight, you will learn how to recognize and recover from stalls. Additionally, you will be introduced to the autopilot and learn to use the autopilot HDG and ALT functions to relieve workload during future flights.

Preflight Discussion

❑ A discussion to introduce the recognition of, procedure for and recovery from the stall series with emphasis on aerodynamics, situational awareness and CFIT concerns.

❑ A discussion to introduce the autopilot HDG and ALT modes and how it relieves cockpit workload.

❑ Ground Scenarios: discovering situations when having the autopilot on makes sense and situations when not to use the autopilot.

Table 3-2

Introduced in this Flight (check your skill level)		DECISION BOX

Explain   Practice

Explain	Practice	
❑	❑	Recovery from Power Off and Approach to Landing Stalls
❑	❑	Recovery from Power On and Takeoff & Departure Stalls

Instructor in flight demonstration:
- ❑ Engage Auto
- ❑ Engage HDG, make heading changes using auto
- ❑ Engage ALT, make altitude changes using auto
- ❑ Engage ALT Preselect, make altitude changes and leveloffs with pre-select
- ❑ Disengage Auto, demonstrating different methods

❑	❑	Student Action – Return to the home airport using HDG and ALT. Make heading changes during radar vectors using HDG. Make altitude changes during radar vectors using ALT.
❑	❑	CFIT Considerations

DECISION BOX
List here decisions the pilot made on this flight

Reviewed from Previous Flights (check your skill level)

Explain	Practice	Perform	Manage	NA	
❑	❑	❑	❑	❑	Did the pilot conduct the preflight correctly without prompting, start, run up, and handle radio communication; taxi to runway?
❑	❑	❑	❑	❑	Positive Exchange of Flight Controls
❑	❑	❑	❑	❑	Normal Takeoff and Climb
❑	❑	❑	❑	❑	Maneuvering During Slow Flight
❑	❑	❑	❑	❑	Straight and Level Flight
❑	❑	❑	❑	❑	Constant Airspeed Climbs and Descents
❑	❑	❑	❑	❑	Normal Approach and Landing
❑	❑	❑	❑	❑	Situational Awareness
❑	❑	❑	❑	❑	Collision Avoidance Precautions

Postflight Discussion

Learner-Centered Grading: ❑ The Pilot   ❑ The Plane
❑ The Environment   ❑ The Operation   ❑ The Situation

❑ Quiz #1: reviewed, corrected to 100% and filed in training record

❑ **Homework** Read Assignment

❑ **Homework** Complete www.asf.org, Free Online Course: GPS for VFR

Completion Standards You will have completed this lesson satisfactorily by MANAGING all aspects of the flight from start to the runway. You will also be able to EXPLAIN the important elements of the stall recognition and recovery. You will PRACTICE controlling the airplane with prompt, positive, smooth and coordinated control manipulation. You will EXPLAIN the use of the autopilot.

_____ _____/_____/_____
I certify this lesson was completed by me. Pilot Signature and Date

_____ _____/_____/_____
I certify this lesson was conducted by me. Instructor Signature and Date

Adapted from King Schools, Inc. Cleared for Takeoff Syllabus.

Which is Preferred?

Whether a full FITS-accepted syllabus or a redesigned syllabus is preferred depends on the instructor, aircraft, pilot, and the training environment.

Instructor: The instructor in a FITS-accepted course is usually either an experienced instructor or a new instructor who is led by a strong Chief Instructor. FITS lessons require careful planning and continuity to ensure the pilot is exposed to the concepts of a scenario before it begins.

Aircraft: FITS-accepted courses excel when the training airplane is equipped with at least a GPS and autopilot. It's unlikely that the FAA would accept a course featuring an airplane that is not equipped with at least GPS and autopilot as a FAA/Industry Training Standard.

Pilot: Pilots enrolled in FITS-accepted course will likely require more hours to solo. This may not be important in a university or ab initio school where all pilots undergo the same training and understand its flow. Otherwise, at a traditional general aviation airport, a FITS course and its longer hours to solo may put an instructor at a competitive disadvantage if airport rumors indicate that the instructor's pilots require more hours to solo. Initial results on the first FITS combined private and instrument course indicate less money and fewer hours are required. Unfortunately, cultural and ego issues require instructors to contend with the conventional impulse to solo with a minimum number of hours.

Training Environment: Scenario-based lessons will take longer to accomplish. Usually the extra time is spent on the ground as the instructor allows the pilot the time needed to discover his own answers in ground scenarios. Schedule .3 to .5 hours additional time over a traditional lesson. Additionally, FITS philosophies require formal ground briefings. Scheduled and strategically placed within the flight curriculum, ground briefings allow the pilot to correlate academic subjects into the process of flying. This is especially important if the pilot's ground training is a self-study or computer-based instruction. The instructor is important in helping the pilot to bring ground academics into the cockpit.

However, while scenario-based lessons are longer, it's also likely that fewer lessons will be required—thus resulting in about the same or fewer hours to graduate.

Conclusions

This chapter introduced the FAA/Industry Training Standards and compared it to conventional flight training. It showed an example of a

FITS-styled lesson plan and compared it to a lesson plan evolved from a generic, commercially-available syllabus. Both incorporated Situational Awareness, Positive Aircraft Control, Risk Management, Aeronautical Decision Making, Automation/Tasks Management, and Controlled Flight into Terrain awareness into pilot training. By understanding how to include these concepts into flight training, the instructor can better decide which syllabus he prefers to teach with.

Exercises

1. Define and discuss technically advanced aircraft.
2. Rewrite a traditional maneuvers-based lesson in full FITS format.
3. Survey and accumulate 25 valuable, free, easily available handouts to support aviation training.

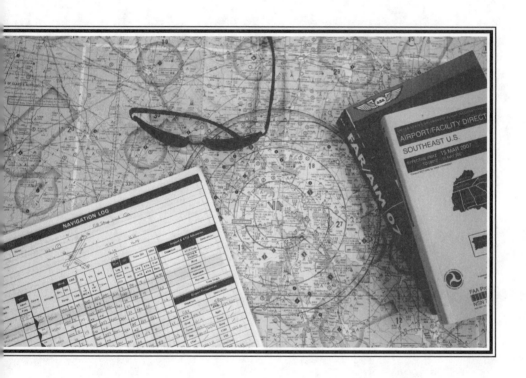

Chapter 4

Debriefing and Evaluating

Better Debriefings

How much is learned during a scenario hinges on the effectiveness of the debriefing. The debriefing gives the pilot time to reflect upon what was a busy training event. The instructor too is afforded feedback on possible additional training the pilot may need—with respect to aircraft control as well as the aeronautical decision-making process.

During the debriefing, the instructor's role is to be a "facilitator of learning rather than the disseminator of knowledge." The FAA Advisory Circular on "Line Operational Simulations (LOS)"[1] suggests that instructors should lead debriefings in a way that encourages pilots to analyze their performance. Rather than lecture to the pilot on what they did right and wrong, the instructor should facilitate the pilot's self-analysis.

"Adult-learning literature suggests that learner-centered grading provides deeper learning and better retention."[2] Learner-centered debriefings may also help pilots develop the habit and skill of analyzing their own performance. This chapter will deal with scenario completion standards, elements to include during a debriefing, and ideas on how to debrief using learner-centered grading or evaluation.

Scenario Completion Standards

A traditional lesson debriefing centers on the pilot's ability to control the aircraft. In scenario-based training, the instructor includes all of the important aspects relating to how well the pilot managed the pilot, the plane, the environment, the operation, and the situation.[3]

A new grading system quantifies how well the pilot commands the entire flight. A scenario grading system evaluates how control for the flight is transferred from the instructor to the pilot (see next page).

Completion Standards

During this lesson you will **perform** all tasks pertaining to aircraft automation including GPS programming and MFD/PFD setup. You will **perform** each of the takeoffs and establish the autopilot climb. En route you will **perform** navigation, programming data link weather operation and power management. You will **practice** manual and coupled ILS instrument approaches, procedure turns, manual and autopilot-assisted missed approaches. You will make all decisions pertaining to the flight and **perform** situational and CFIT awareness.

To grade the elements of a scenario requires something more than a "needs improvement" evaluation system; FITS gives us a needed, new system. FITS grades replace the traditional A, B, C academic grades or the "meets standards" grade that traditionally assessed how well the pilot completed a maneuver.

The FITS grades are designed to incorporate the pilot's thinking skills as well as the maneuver being flown. But in the FITS learner-centered grading document the reader finds that these grades differ slightly, depending upon whether the grade is given for a maneuver or flight management role. It's a little complicated but can be simplified with the following format:

Describe: This lowest grade is achieved when the pilot is able to **describe** the learning task. For example, the pilot may know what to do, but not when to do it. The lowest grade should not be interpreted as a failing grade, rather that the pilot has achieved the first level.

Explain: If the pilot is able to **explain** the activity and its concepts, he gets a higher grade. For instance if at 3,000 AGL the instructor asks for a turn about a point and the pilot explains that he must establish the correct altitude before beginning the maneuver, a higher grade is warranted.

Practice: If the pilot is able to **practice** the activity, it is assumed that the instructor is still needed as a coach. If the pilot's landings are improving but the instructor must still prompt for more rudder during crosswind, the pilot is at this level.

Perform: If the pilot is able to **perform** the activity, it's assumed that errors are caught and corrected by the pilot. This grade parallels satisfactory performance in traditional training programs. Responsibility for airplane control has been fully transferred from the instructor to the pilot. This is the point at which most instructors stop teaching. But there is more.

Manage/Decide: When the pilot is able to gather the most important data, identify different possible alternatives, evaluate the risk in each and make the best decision, then the pilot is able to **manage** and **describe** all aspects of the flight. This is the highest grade. This signifies that the pilot has full situational awareness and is able to put it all together as the sole pilot-in-command. **Manage/decide** defines proficiency in the single-pilot resource management area.

Considering the four levels of learning, rote is closely associated to **explain**, understanding is closely related to **practice**, application can be thought of as **perform**, and correlation defines the pilot at the **manage/decide** grade.

At any point in training, any grade could be satisfactory. For example, during the second flight it would be acceptable for the pilot to be at the **describe** level on landings. But if the pilot is still at the **describe** level nearing solo, it would not be acceptable. At any point, each level could be considered a passing grade, or not. The grading system is designed for both pilot and instructor to see progress made as the pilot prepares to be in command.

While satisfactory completion is a desirable aspect of any training, it's hard to imagine unsatisfactory training if learning was accomplished. Even a scenario that results in a simulated "crash" is still a satisfactory lesson because the pilot logged valuable experience and was able to **explain** what not to do again.

What to Grade

The objective is to get the pilot to the point where he can **manage** the entire flight. On most flights, this includes managing the pilot, the plane, the environment, the operation and the situation.

In discussions relating to the "pilot," consider how well the pilot **managed** his fatigue, stress, medications, hazardous attitudes and other items traditionally included on the I'M SAFE checklist.

In discussions relating to the plane, consider how well the pilot **managed** the aircraft's performance, equipment, avionics, fuel reserves, and airworthiness, etc.

In discussions relating to the environment, consider how well the pilot **managed** staying clear of weather, the runway and airport conditions, ATC clearances and other external and environmental factors.

In discussions relating to the operation, consider how well the pilot managed the interaction of the pilot flying the plane in its environment. The operation includes the task or maneuver being completed, not only in terms of practical test standards, but in managing the risk associated with the total operation. Did the pilot elect to perform a stall while at 500 feet AGL? If so, he probably didn't **manage** the operation because the instructor had to intervene.

In discussions relating to the situation, consider how well the pilot **managed** his situational awareness. The situation considers how the four items above interact, what alternatives may be available to the pilot to improve the situation or the appropriateness of discontinuing the flight.

Learner-Centered Grading

Self-evaluation is an important part of scenario-based training. The *Aviation Instructor's Handbook* speaks about "Student-Led Critique" and "Self-Critique." FITS recognizes "Learner Centered Grading" while traditional scenario-based educators refer to "facilitating" as a way to evaluate student performance. Each of these techniques are similar in that they attempt to involve the pilot in additional learning opportunities often revealed during the debrief process.[4]

Self-evaluation shines light on the thinking process of the pilot. While the pilot's proficiency at flying a maneuver is evident, the instructor can't see what's going on inside the pilot's head. Self-evaluation allows the instructor to discern what the pilot is thinking and how the pilot lines up his priorities.

During the scenario debriefing, the instructor guides a dialogue into areas that need discussion. The dialogue includes questions about procedures, decisions, and mistakes. The pilot is asked to engage in the debriefing. But this is not the place for an instructor's "lecture."

One debriefing format that works well is:

- **Open the Discussion.** Make a positive general statement to begin.
- **Discuss the Scenario.** Encourage the pilot to discuss the scenario both as a whole and in parts. The traditional way to organize the debriefing is to replay the scenario step by step. Another way to organize the debriefing is to relate information to The Pilot, The Plane, The Environment, The Operation and The Situation.
- **Offer Alternatives.** Perhaps the pilot didn't recognize or consider another option.
- **Ask Questions.** Develop the discussion more fully. "What if…?" is a useful question.
- **Summarize.** Emphasize the positive learning that was accomplished and how the pilot can apply what they learned in the scenario to real flying. If the scenario was realistic, this should be easy to do.

Using student-centered learning does not eliminate the need for an instructor. At times, traditional instructing will be needed when information is transferred from instructor to student. At other times facilitating should be the focus when the instructor's role is encouraging pilot self-discovery. The instructor must be willing and ready to alternate between the two roles.

FITS suggests that grading be conducted by the student, then by the instructor, and then the two grades are compared. But this doesn't imply that learner-centered grading is done separately. The debrief should be a dialogue between the pilot and instructor. Consider the following sample debriefing from *Facilitating LOS Debriefings: A Training Manual*.[5]

Set the Scene and Open a Dialogue

"Okay, we made a lot of progress today. Why don't you replay the flight for us?" Or,

"I'm pleased. That went well. Would you like to start by recapping the high points?"

Lead Into the Areas Needing Discussion

Effective

CFI: "What else about how we handled that emergency situation can we discuss?"

Pilot: "Well, now that you mention it, I did get a little rushed…"

Ineffective

CFI: "Did you get a little rushed in that emergency situation?"

Pilot: "Yeah, I did."

Deepen the Pilot's Consideration

Effective

> CFI: "Was there anything else that made you uncomfortable in that first leg?"
>
> Pilot: "Ah, no I don't…"
>
> CFI: "How did you feel about that first approach?"
>
> Pilot: "Ah…yeah, I was uncomfortable about being at an airport with so many runways."

Ineffective

> CFI: "You seemed a little uncomfortable being at the large airport. Were you?"
>
> Pilot: "Yeah."

Resolve Pilot Concerns

Effective

> Pilot: "I think I should fly at only the smaller fields until I get more experience."
>
> CFI: "Let's talk about that. What could we have done to be better prepared to fly in that environment?"
>
> Pilot: "Well, if I'd studied the airport diagram before the flight I would have been better prepared. I guess I should have anticipated the winds and what the active runway would be. Assuming what the active runway would be, I could have anticipated how to transition from enroute into the traffic pattern for the active runway."

Ineffective

> Pilot: "I think I should fly at only the smaller fields until I get more experience."
>
> CFI: "Yeah, the FAA makes us do three takeoffs and landings at a controlled field. But you've got it behind you now and you never have to go back there if you don't want to."

Turn Questions Back to Them

Effective

> Pilot: "I don't know what happened there, was I going too fast?"
>
> CFI: "Was your approach speed too fast?"
>
>> Pilot: "No, the speed was the right speed, it's just that by the time I got the power adjusted, the flaps in, the trim done and talked to the tower I didn't have time to complete the prelanding checklist and forgot to turn on the fuel pump."

Ineffective

> Pilot: "I don't know what happened there, was I going too fast?"
> CFI: "No, your speed was just fine, but you were talking to ATC when you should have been completing the checklist."

When the Pilot Does Not Participate

Effective

> CFI: "Has there ever been a flight when the pilot made zero mistakes?"
> Pilot: "No."
> CFI: "And what do we want to have happen when mistakes are made?"

(The CFI allows about 10 seconds of silence if the pilot doesn't respond immediately. Give the pilot time to think.)

> Pilot: "We want to correct the mistake."
> CFI: "That's right."

Ineffective

> CFI: "Has there ever been a flight when the pilot made zero mistakes?"
> Pilot: "No."
> CFI "And what do we want to have happen when mistakes are made?"

(The CFI becomes uncomfortable when the pilot doesn't answer immediately and the CFI answers for him.)

> CFI: "We want to correct the mistake, right?"

Summary

Debriefing a scenario takes longer than debriefing a traditional lesson. There is more to talk about. Properly including the concepts of The Pilot, The Plane, The Environment, The Operation, and The Situation go well beyond the normal debrief. Extra time is required to allow the pilot to think through the underlying concepts and to discover for himself how he should best react to a situation. Don't be afraid of silent moments to allow the pilot to think. Don't rush the pilot through the discovery process—this is where the real aeronautical decision making is learned by the pilot and becomes internalized instead of simply being words on paper. This is when the pilot accepts on the personal level how he will react to various situations and his propensity for a hazardous attitude. This is where scenario-based training really shines. Instructors should schedule an extra 15 to 20 minutes over the usual time required for a scenario debrief.

Throughout the debriefing, the scenario must be perceived as not just an hour of flight, but a valuable experience. Begin each scenario debriefing with enthusiasm for the experience. Focus on the decision making and resource management of the pilot. Evaluate how well the pilot made use of alternative actions, all available options, and onboard cockpit equipment such as autopilot and other workload-reducing devices.

Conclusions

New lesson completion standards including a new grading system and debriefing methodology were introduced in this chapter. Assuming that most people who engage in flight training are adults, the concept of learner-centered grading was introduced as the preferred method for a scenario-based debriefing. Lastly, the debriefing was broken into elements of: The Pilot, The Plane, The Environment, The Operation, and The Situation.

Exercises

1. Download *Facilitating LOS Debriefings: A Training Manual* from where it is linked on the ASA website at **http://www.asa2fly.com/trainfly**. Read the document, paying specific attention to the examples of effective and ineffective debriefing. Give examples on how you could adapt the examples in this document for your own use with your pilots

2. Using the scenarios that you wrote in Chapter 2, further define and expand the debrief section to include a script to be added to your "tool box."

Chapter 5

Instrument Scenario Training

The elements of training a good instrument pilot are the same as pilot training in the basics:
- *Apply aeronautical knowledge in the cockpit while flying;*
- *Correlate individual tasks into a bigger picture;*
- *Place the pilot in command of as much of the flight as possible as quickly as possible;*
- *Allow the pilot to make mistakes in a controlled environment and build the pilot's abilities in situational awareness.*

This chapter will look at scenarios used in training the instrument pilot, the benefits of training in devices and using structured scripted scenarios.

Aviation Training Devices

In the instrument course, the instructor may choose to use an aviation training device (ATD). Recent studies have thus far been unable to verify significant cost savings for pilots training in devices over training in an airplane.[1] However, ATDs provide flexibility by permitting a pilot to practice on a particular make of airplane, to see a graphic display of their performance, and to fly under varying flight situations: instrument failures, ATC requests and weather conditions.

ATDs can be effective in teaching more than procedures, if you incorporate the use of scenarios. Scenarios allow devices to be used effectively to teach the higher-thinking skills needed by instrument pilots. Scenarios conducted in the device may also increase pilot interest for additional training, as you expand the instrument training to include procedures in real-time practice.

Instrument Maneuvers for Beginning Skills

Vertical S

The Vertical S is a maneuver that assembles the basic instrument-attitudes into a single maneuver. Should the pilot become bored with practice of standard rate turns and constant airspeed climbs, the Vertical S makes practice more exciting. It requires the pilot to not only manage precise control of the device, but to think ahead and to maintain situational awareness by tracking his progress through the predetermined sequence. (See Figure 5-1.)

Pattern A and B

Pattern A and B are diagramed procedures requiring the pilot to read instructions and include the diagram in his scan. It is the pilot's first exposure to diagrammed instructions that require a sequential flow of procedures. It also requires the pilot to use proper timing to complete a series of maneuvers resembling a holding pattern and procedure turn. Once the pilot has mastered the procedure, then the instructor can dial up some turbulence in the ATD, or go partial panel in the airplane. (See Figure 5-2 on page 70.)

Scenario for Incorporating Technology

The time to introduce technology is after the pilot has become proficient in basic instrument attitudes. Introduce the autopilot first, if installed. It provides the pilot the option of having the autopilot control the airplane while the GPS is being introduced. Don't overwhelm the pilot with all the functions all at once. Introduce the simplest functions first and then add additional functions during subsequent lessons.

During this scenario, the pilot uses Page Groups required for IFR departure, en route and approach (the collections of "pages" or menus in a GPS unit). Simultaneously, the pilot controls the aircraft in the automated mode of a G1000-equipped technically advanced aircraft.

> The mission departs a Class C Airport. The pilot will **manage** programming of com frequencies for ATIS, ground, tower and departure control as well as programming a flight plan to Campbellsville, KY (KAAS). He will use traditional charts to determine an appropriate safe altitude with emphasis on terrain and obstacle clearance. En route the pilot will **practice** use of checklists, programming the G1000, lean assist and VNAV descent. The pilot will **perform** a VOR/DME-A approach; activated and executed using the DME arc. The pilot will program the AWOS, determine which runway to circle for landing and **perform** the circle procedure. This will require monitoring of UNICOM. When the pilot determines that all requirements have been met

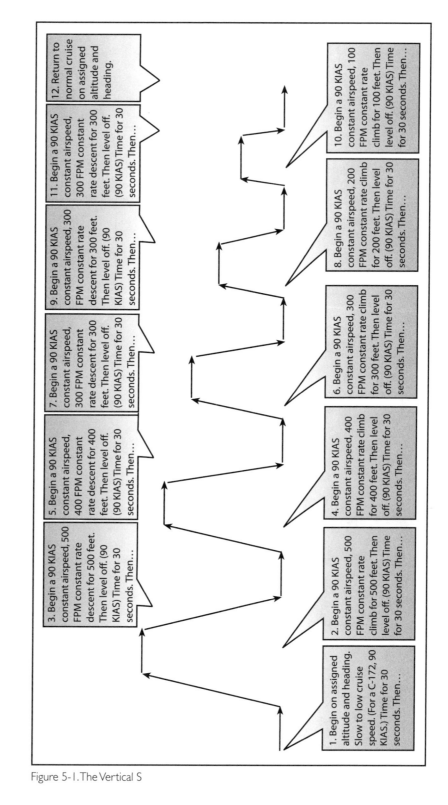

Figure 5-1. The Vertical S

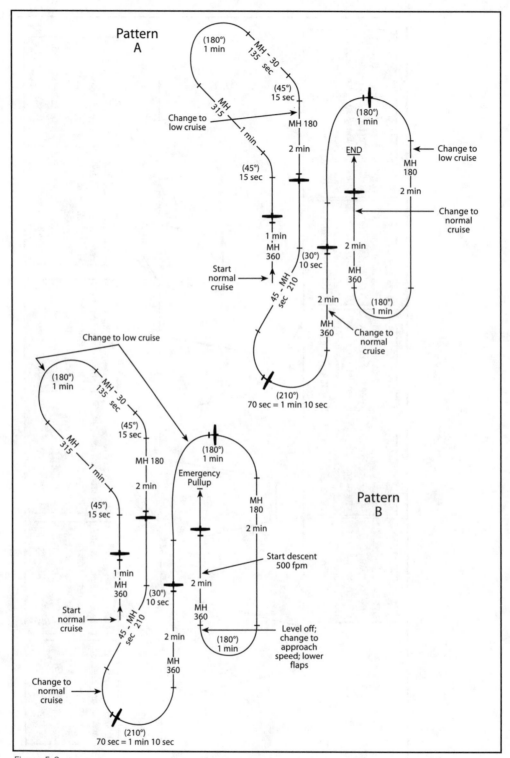

Figure 5-2

to descend below MDA, he will execute a full stop landing. The pilot may decide to taxi back for departure or to shutdown for debriefing before beginning the next leg. Flight time on this leg is 30 minutes.

The pilot will enter a flight plan from KAAS to NITDO intersection, then to Clark Co, IN (KJVY). NITDO will allow circumnavigation of the busy Louisville "C" Airspace. One objective on this leg is to correlate TIS indications with traffic viewed from the cockpit. The pilot will review traditional charts/references to decide on an appropriate safe altitude. En route the pilot will **practice** use of checklists, programming the G-1000, lean assist and VNAV descent as the single pilot on board. The pilot will maintain situational awareness to **manage** and avoid "C" airspace. At the pilot's discretion, he will activate and execute a fully-automated ILS using the CATCH IAF. When the pilot determines that all requirements have been met to descend below DA, he will execute a full stop landing. The pilot may decide to taxi back for departure or to shutdown for debriefing before beginning the next leg. Flight time on this leg is 40 minutes.

As much as possible, provide opportunities for the pilot to make decisions during the flight. Make it obvious that the pilot is expected to make decisions and to control as much of the flight as possible using the technology and operating as the sole pilot on board.

Fully Scripted Scenarios

Fully scripted scenarios require a great deal of time and effort to construct, but they offer the benefit of maximum guidance for both pilot and instructor in complicated situations.

Instructors are generally disciplined to remain diligent and alert in an airplane. But working on the ground in an ATD, the pilot busily **manages** the flight, soon feels akin to a spectator. Fully scripted scenarios ensure that the instructor stays involved and on track with what the pilot is doing. It serves as an outline of items to supervise. The script allows the instructor to participate in the scenario, acting in the role of ATC controller, FSS and the cast of other players required to add realism to the "flight."

The fully scripted scenario can include a special page of instructions for the pilot. By assigning the scenario to the pilot in advance, it allows the pilot to mentally prepare for the flight and to make mental preflight preparations much in the same way he would preflight in the real airplane.

With realism being the underlying theme of any scenario, the use of actual, current instrument charts and procedures must be used in both ATDs and in flight scenarios.

Scripted Scenarios

The HYK VOR Flight Scenario shown at the end of this chapter (see Page 77) is introduced in either the airplane or ATD, usually after the pilot has learned to **manage** basic aircraft control. In this scenario, the pilot is asked to navigate using an L-chart and to use a clock while controlling the airplane; the objective being to combine the elements. This provides a prelude to VOR approaches and the circling maneuver. The script includes a pilot information page that the instructor uses to brief the pilot on scenario particulars. The scenario requires the pilot to prepare by completing assigned homework. The instructor's script and evaluation outline leads the instructor in keeping control of the scenario and is filed in the pilot's training record as evidence of training.

The DNY.BDR1 Arrival Scenario is introduced after the pilot has been exposed to holding. In the ATD, the pilot departs from an uncontrolled airport on a void time clearance and navigates using the 55 NM Bridgeport Arrival. The scenario includes three separate holds and ends with a VOR Approach. It's a good example of effectively using the ATD to get the pilot out of his home area and into unknown airspace and terrain.

The Gallatin to Bowling Green Scenario is an example of a scenario that gives the pilot the opportunity to practice decision-making skills while dealing with routine but unexpected events. It features a void time clearance, a departure procedure, nonradar position report, a hold, an amended clearance, a cruise clearance, VOR/DME instrument approach procedure, a missed approach in low night IMC, an ILS to minimums, and a crosswind landing. It is normally introduced as soon as the pilot is able to **manage** routine instrument procedures, but before the instrument cross-country phase of training. See all these scenarios at the end of this chapter starting on Page 77.

Organizing a Library of Scripts

Instructors seasoned in scenario training collect a library of tested scripts. Organizing a large library becomes problematic. The preferred method of organization divides scripts into categories by pilot ability. Typically during training, the pilot is expected to advance from the simpler scenarios to the more difficult.

First Look Scenarios are generally simple scenarios of about 30 minutes without heavy weather or mechanical failures. First look scenarios allow the pilot to become accustomed with the aviation training device and its equipment while refreshing basic instrument skills. It provides the instructor a first look at the pilot's abilities. Generally, instructors need only a few first look scenarios.

Opportunity Scenarios are normally more difficult and slightly longer in duration. They provide opportunities for the pilot to practice instrument procedures in unexpected but routine elements of instrument flying. They provide the instructor with the opportunity to evaluate the pilot's headwork. Performance from this session is used to determine the extent to which decision-making process may need to be introduced by the instructor. They also provide a baseline for assessing improvement. The largest selection of scripted scenarios will be in the opportunity category as new instrument pilots are learning procedures and IPC candidates are re-learning techniques. Opportunity scenarios should remove the pilot from familiar terrain and airspace, giving him the opportunity to experience new simulated scenery and new skills.

Challenge Scenarios push the pilot into full cross-country mode with full weather data. Challenge scenarios require a great deal of preparation by the pilot who is expected to evaluate the weather, make the flight plan, complete a Navlog, conduct the flight and deal with adversities and failures. Challenge scenarios are so effective that the pilot need only fly one or two to get the ideas of cockpit organization, situational awareness and single-pilot control. Instructors will need only two or three challenge scenarios.

The Instructor's Role

The instructor must have previously flown and rehearsed the scenario before attempting to teach with it. Done correctly, it's a busy lesson for the instructor—supervising what the pilot is doing and preparing for his next cue. The better the script, the easier the instructor's job and the more effective the lesson will be.

The instructor must be prepared to play all the supporting roles necessary to facilitate the scenario. The instructor may be in the role of FSS giving an IFR clearance void-time at the start, only to become ATC as the pilot enters controlled airspace en route and then AWOS upon arriving at the destination. The instructor must intuitively understand which role is being played and the limitations of that cast member. Sterile cockpit procedures must prevail for the pilot. There should be no interaction between the "instructor" and the pilot unless absolutely necessary to progress the scenario forward.

The instructor must be able to speak in a formal tone of voice and in proper pilot/controller phraseology when issuing "clearances." Make it feel and sound real. Consider having your scripted scenarios scrutinized by a local ATC controller.

The instructor must be prepared for the unexpected. Once the pilot has been given the scenario, the instructor must be ready to go with the decisions of the pilot. At times, the instructor may be called upon to ad-lib when the decisions of the pilot were unanticipated and unscripted. Instructors must curtail the temptation to help the pilot. However, a creative instructor can control the boundaries of the scenario through unexpected "ATC clearances" or equipment failures.

Training Device Programming

Curtail the temptation to hit the pause button. Scenarios must be allowed to continue in real time. The flight must be ended with a landing at an airport somewhere, just as it would be in real life. Resist the urge to indulge in unrealistic situations. Surface winds in excess of 28 knots, winds aloft in excess of what is appropriate and multiple simultaneous failures are some examples of unproductive factors.

Set the programming to allow the pilot to be "on top" and in the sunshine for a portion of the flight. Allow breaks in the clouds and multiple layers. "Hard" IFR that begins 200 feet AGL and continues until near DH is not realistic. A pilot flying in and out of clouds is given one additional distraction to deal with. If the ATD can be programmed, program the time of day to be dusk rather than dark black night. The single pilot IFR accident rate during nighttime is almost 8 times the accident rate of day IFR approaches and 2.5 times the accident rate of day VFR approaches.[2]

Assuming the ATD has a full U.S. database, use the opportunity to engage the pilot in interesting or unique approaches from around the country. Consider the actual, interesting approaches, DPs, and STARs shown in Table 5-1.

Table 5-1. Interesting approaches for use in ATD scenarios.

Watertown, NY	ILS RWY 7	Most interesting when the full approach is flown. Will the pilot be able to determine how far outbound to fly before returning inbound? The trick is to go far enough out so that the glide slope is intercepted from below. Prevailing winds guarantee a tailwind ILS. The missed approach hold is also fun. Program the ATD for the typical wind from the west or northwest.
Fulton, NY	ILS RWY 33	A 4.35 degree glide slope. Will the pilot notice it during his normal approach plate brief?
Cortland, NY	VOR-A	A very long approach course ending in a circle maneuver. The pilot must lose 1,500 feet of altitude over 4 miles after the FAF. The MAP is directly over the airport runway and 82 feet above traffic pattern altitude, which is usually missed when the pilot pulls up the foggles.
Jackson Hole, WY		A lot of mountains, doglegs and high density altitude.
Altoona, PA	WILT 3 DP Tates 3 DP	Steep mountains during climb out. Beautiful scenery for those ATDs so equipped.
Eagle, CO, Eagle County Regional	GYPSUM 3 DP	Few aircraft meet this climb gradient. The route appears to circle around the VOR because after the first turn, the VOR elevation is still above you.
KJFK	VOR RWY 13L/13R	This one keeps a pilot busy!
Casper, WY Natrona County	VOR/DME or TACAN RWY 21	More interesting than difficult.
Portsmouth/Pease International Tradeport in Portsmouth, NH	GPS RWY 16	The intersection names remind you of tweedy bird from Warner Brothers. "I tawt I taw a puddee tat".
Bellingham, WA	ILS RWY16	Go to the VOR and intercept the transition route. It's an exercise in avionics management, switching from the VOR, ADF, then to the ILS; with a procedure turn thrown in for good measure.
Butte, MT	VOR-GPS-B	A DME arc and a heading change at the FAF keeps pilots on their toes.

The Real Thing

Of course, best of all is the real thing. Instrument pilots should be exposed to flight in actual instrument conditions—about 10 hours of actual cloud time will ensure the pilot's confidence for flight in the clouds after graduation.

Use a series of short cross-countries to teach decision making. Use longer cross-countries to award the pilot opportunities to fly in various weather patterns and in new airspace. In some instances, multiple pilots can be included in the training flight. On a long cross-country, pilots can alternate from back seat to left seat to trade off flying duties. Get pilots to fly farther and split the cost of the lesson. For instance, an instructor may orchestrate a several-hundred-mile fall foliage tour of New England states, a pre-Christmas shopping spree at the Minneapolis Mall of the Americas or a Spring Break snow skiing trip to the mountains of Colorado.

Instrument Regulation Scenario

The Federal Aviation Regulations should not be a stand-alone subject taught separately. Introduce regulations as they impact the flight. Discuss regulations as they pertain to the mission. Look for new ways to relate regulations to the flight when designing scenarios. During oral exams and ground briefings, relate regulations in the context of a typical flight so that the pilot learns to apply the requirements to a real flight.

Conclusions

Today's busy airspace presents problems for many pilots, especially those training at uncontrolled fields. The airplanes are traveling faster, ATC is talking fast, and the pilot is expected to think fast to stay ahead of it all. Simulating a realistic ATC environment is the highest objective in instrument training.

Using fully scripted scenarios allows the instructor to fully control all aspects of a busy flight lesson. By incorporating regulations into realistic scenarios, the instructor is assured that the pilot is able to correctly apply these concepts in real life. A carefully organized library of scripts provides the instructor with ready-made tools for effective instrument instruction.

Exercises

1. Using the LEX Intersection Scenario as your example, design a similar scenario for your local training environment.
2. Using the K24 GPS Scenario as your example, design a similar scenario for your aircraft technology and an airport in your local area.
3. Using the DNY.BDR1 Scenario as your example, design a similar scenario using a different chart to teach a hold. Remember to script your communication.

Sample Scripted Scenarios

HYK VOR Flight Scenario   Pilot's Information Page

Give this page to the pilot.

Objective: An instrument flight combining basic instrument attitude flying, cockpit organization and navigation skills. This scenario will last about 1 hour.

Materials: Aircraft checklist, kneeboard and L chart. You are encouraged to use all available cockpit resources.

Pilot Briefing:

You are expected to MANAGE all aspects of engine start, taxi and takeoff. You will speak to "ATC." You are expected to PERFORM VOR navigation while MANAGING constant rate, constant airspeed climbs and descents, standard rate turns. You will fly direct to the VOR, identify VOR intersections, and reset your cockpit NAVAIDS to complete the round-robin back into KLEX. You will be required to time certain aspects of the flight.

If in the ATD, conduct this flight as you would in the actual airplane. The instructor will familiarize you with the cockpit technology and button-ology. He may help you choose to stop the navigation portion of the lesson if you are experiencing difficulty controlling the "airplane." If the scenario is not challenging to you, he may also choose to increase the level of turbulence.

Emphasis is placed on smoothness in aircraft control, attitude flying and thinking ahead. To perform well on this flight requires strong basic attitude-instrument skills. Organize your cockpit because there is a lot happening in this lesson with navaid changeovers and intersection identification while flying. Think ahead of the plane. Study the chart and envision how you will navigate. Notice the MEA changes. Make sure you understand the mission. The pace of the scenario should provide ample rest. It's steady but unrushed.

Your Clearance:

(N-number), cleared round-robin to LEX, direct HYK, V53 to IRVINE, V517 to CODEL V4 to HYK. Climb to and maintain two thousand five hundred. Departure 120.75, squawk 7227.

- Reaching assigned altitude, slow to 90 KIAS and remain at 90 until further advised. Thence...
- After HYK, begin a 90 KIAS, 500 FPM climb to MEA.
- After IRVINE, begin a 90 KIAS, 500 FPM climb to 3,500.
- Crossing LOGIC, the artificial horizon instrument fails.

- Crossing LOGIC, begin a 90 KIAS 500 FPM descent to MEA.
- Crossing CODEL, join V4, to HYK. Begin 90 KIAS appropriate FPM climb to 3,000.
- After crossing HYK, proceed outbound on the R-305 and begin a 500 FPM descent for a period of 4 minutes
- Circle to land.
- (If in the ATD) Weather is: 1,000 BKN, rain, 2 SM visibility, surface winds 300/15 at 3,000 feet, 310/25. Where do you expect to be in relation to the clouds?
- Time is: Sunset, dusk going into dark.

Get into the role, play the game and have fun. This is high-level training. Expect to make errors in your decision-making and expect to learn from the experience. Tailwinds and safe landing.

The end of pilot information for this scenario.

HYK VOR Flight Scenario   Instructor Script and Evaluation Outline (2 Pages)

Preflight Briefing – elements: Identification of intersections and navaid set up, proper timing, aspects of the circling maneuver.

Pilot's Name	Date / /

Engine Start

❏ Does the pilot perform checklists?

❏ Does the pilot correctly start "aircraft" and perform run-up?

❏ Wait for pilot to dial in ATIS frequency, then ATIS says: "…ceiling one thousand six hundred overcast. Temp ture 22, dewpoint 20, altimeter 29.92. ILS Runway 4 in use. Landing and departing Runway 22. Read back all runway cross- ing and runway hold short instructions. Advise on initial contact you have information Sierra. Lexington Blue Grass Airport Information Sierra, time 0000Z (use local time). Wind 300 at one five gusts to one eight. Visibility three rain, …" (Keep repeating without break until pilot changes frequency)

❏ Clearance Delivery says: "(N-Number), cleared round-robin to LEX, direct HYK, V53 to IRVINE, V517 to CODEL V4 to HYK. Climb and maintain two thousand five hundred. Departure 120.75, squawk 7227."

❏ Does the pilot call for and correctly read back ATC clearance?

❏ When pilot calls ready for takeoff, Tower says: (N-number), fly runway heading, Runway 4, cleared for immediate takeoff or hold short – RJ on 2 mile final."

❏ Does the pilot choose an "immediate takeoff"?

❏ Does the pilot record takeoff time?

❏ Does the pilot pre-program cockpit technology before takeoff rather than to be distracted by button-ology after takeoff?

❏ Does the pilot perform takeoff with proper crosswind correction? Was pilot aware of crosswind?

❏ Was takeoff time recorded?

❏ Does the pilot observe takeoff procedure and comply?
        (DP = Climb runway heading to 1,400 MSL before turning)

❏ At 1,400 feet MSL, Tower Says: "(N-Number), Contact Departure 120.75."

❏ When pilot contacts departure, Departure says: "(N-Number) Radar contact, climb to two thousand five hundred, cleared direct HYK."

❏ Does the pilot engage autopilot shortly after cruise-climb and fully use cockpit resources?

Cruise

❏ Cruise climb, proper level-off and leaning?

❏ Does the pilot properly establish on-course, at cruise altitude?

❏ Does the pilot slow to 90 KIAS efficiently?

❏ Instructor action: After HYK remind pilot to begin 90 KIAS, 500 FPM climb to MEA (MEA is 3000)

❏ Does the pilot make a smooth attitude transition to climb? Maintain 90 KIAS? Level off after climb, smoothly at 90 KIAS?

❏ Does the pilot reset NAVs for next navigational leg?

❏ Instructor action: After IRVINE remind pilot to begin 90 KIAS, 500 FPM climb to 3,500 (MEA is 3300)

❏ Instructor action: Ensure ATD time of day is lapsing into sunset

❏ Does the pilot turn on cockpit internal and external lights?

❏ Does the pilot make a smooth attitude transition to climb? Maintain 90 KIAS? Level off smoothly at 90 KIAS?

❏ Does the pilot reset NAVs for next leg?

Continued

❏ Instructor action: Crossing LOGIC fail artificial horizon instrument (If in traditional cockpit)
❏ Does the pilot make a smooth attitude transition to partial panel?
❏ Does the pilot check circuit breakers?
❏ Does the pilot reset NAVs?

❏ Instructor action: Crossing LOGIC remind pilot to begin 90 KIAS 500 FPM descent to MEA (MEA is 2800)
❏ Instructor action: If the pilot does not seem to be challenged, increase the ATD level of turbulence up 1 level.
❏ Does the pilot make a smooth attitude transition to descend? Maintain 90 KIAS? Level off smoothly at 90 KIAS?
❏ Does the pilot reset NAVs?

❏ Instructor action: Crossing CODEL remind pilot to join V4 to HYK. Begin 90 KIAS appropriate FPM climb to 3000.
❏ Does pilot make a smooth attitude transition to descend? Maintain 90 KIAS? Level off smoothly at 90 KIAS?
❏ Does pilot reset NAVs?

❏ Instructor action: Ensure ATD time of day is fully dark.

Approach

❏ 2 DME from HYK Lexington Approach says, "(N-number), Radar Contact, cleared direct to HYK. Cleared VOR-A Approach, circle southwest for Runway 4."
❏ Crossing HYK Inbound, Approach Says, "(N-number), Contact Lexington Tower 119.1"
❏ When pilot contacts tower, Tower says: "(N-Number), continue. Expect Runway 4."
❏ Does the pilot properly execute procedure turn and full approach using autopilot?
❏ When pilot crosses DME step down, Tower says, "(N-number) Caution wake turbulence departing 737, runway 4, cleared to land."
❏ Does the pilot use lowest minimums for DME stepdown?

Landing

❏ Does the pilot perform prelanding checklist?
❏ Does the pilot properly execute circling maneuver to proper runway? Leave MDA properly? Remain close in?
❏ Does the pilot use crosswind landing technique? On centerline? Avoid wake turbulence?
❏ After landing, did the pilot not attempt to program flaps, radios or after-landing tasks until clear of runway and full stop?
❏ Does the pilot shutdown using checklists?

Overall, did the pilot:

- ❏ Have a plan in mind before flight to handle each aspect of the flight with special consideration given to managing risks inherent in the flight, cockpit resources management and situational awareness?
- ❏ Make appropriate decisions during the flight?
- ❏ Use his technology?
- ❏ Prioritize cockpit tasks?
- ❏ Remain in control and in command?

During partial panel:

- ❏ Did the pilot quickly recognize the situation? (That he had a failure condition.)
- ❏ Attempt to verify situation and analyze possible corrective action?
- ❏ Make standard rate or half-standard rate turns while partial panel?
- ❏ Demonstrate good skills and awareness of controlled flight into terrain?

Have the pilot explain the scenario activity and the underlying concepts, principals and procedures within the scenario as a self-debrief. Record additional notes on back. File in Pilot's Training Record.

K24 GPS Scenario   Pilot's Information Page

Give this page to the pilot.

Objective: The first portion of this flight introduces the pilot to all aspects of cockpit technology while flying from LEX to K24. Combines use of autopilot, instrument attitude flying, cockpit organization and navigation skills. This scenario will last about 2.5 hours. During flight, the instructor will allow the pilot to conduct the flight as the sole pilot on board. Full use of the autopilot is encouraged.

Materials: Pilot will need an L chart and a K24 GPS 17 and K24 GPS 35 IAP in the cockpit.

Pilot Briefing:

The instructor will fully brief the pilot on the sequence of the flight, the cockpit button-ology required and the thought processes required for success. Cockpit organization and thinking ahead is emphasized. Make sure the pilot fully understands the mission.

The mission is as follows:

- Before takeoff, load a GPS flight plan: LEX UNCLE DOLLY FIBKE K24.
- Cleared to 4,500 MSL.
- When able: DIRECT to UNCLE.
- Once established on course to UNCLE, settled in and under control, REMOVE DOLLY from the flight plan.
- Immediately prior to UNCLE, load LOZ VOR into the flight plan as a waypoint after UNCLE.
- After UNCLE, select NRST airport in case we have to divert, review the airport information.
- Load AWOS frequency into GPS, listen to AWOS of NRST airport (DVK).
- Halfway to LOZ, "Intercept 260-degree course to FIBKE" (this requires OBS mode).
- Enroute to FIBKE, load the K24 GPS 17 with NEYIT IA.
- Crossing FIBKE, activate the approach.
- Conduct the approach and the published missed.
- The published missed requires a hold at TEYOS. Establish the hold.
- After 2X in holding, then load K24 GPS 35 with TEYOS as IAF.
- Conduct the approach with a circle to land Runway 17.

Land at K24, rest, debrief as necessary. Upon returning to KLEX, practice VFR maneuvers. Conduct a GPS approach into KLEX if additional practice is necessary. Otherwise, a fully coupled ILS to a full stop is preferred.

The end of pilot information for this scenario.

Scenario K24 GPS   **Instructor Script and Evaluation Outline (2 Pages)**

Instructor: Make notes on this outline for pilot debriefing. File these notes in Pilot Training Record.

Pilot's Name	Date / /

Engine Start

❏ Does the pilot perform checklists, start, and perform run-up?

❏ Does the pilot know how to load a flight plan?

❏ Does the pilot check RAIM?

❏ Does the pilot perform takeoff with proper crosswind correction?

❏ Was takeoff time recorded?

❏ Does the pilot engage autopilot promptly after cruise-climb and fully use cockpit resources?

To UNCLE

❏ Does the pilot use proper after takeoff, cruise climb, level off and leaning procedures?

❏ Does the pilot properly establish on-course and cruise altitude?

❏ Instructor says: "Go direct to UNCLE."

❏ Does pilot go in to flight plan, highlight UNCLE and press Direct To?

❏ Halfway to UNCLE, Instructor says: "Remove DOLLY from the flight plan" (or ATC can issue a re-route to London VOR).

❏ Immediately prior to UNCLE, Instructor says: "Load London VOR into the flight plan as a waypoint after UNCLE."

To LOZ

❏ Instructor says: "Find our NRST airport. Is that a suitable airport for us?"

❏ Does the pilot load the airport data?

❏ Instructor says: "What's the weather there?"

❏ Does the pilot load AWOS frequency and listen to AWOS (nearest airport is DVK)?

❏ Halfway to LOZ Instructor says: "Intercept 260 degree course to FIBKE. Proceed to FIBKE via the 260."

  o Did pilot switch to OBS mode and properly set up?

To FIBKE

❏ En route to FIBKE, Instructor says: "Load the K24 GPS 17 with NEYIT IAF."

❏ Over FIBKE Instructor says: "Activate the approach."

GPS 17 Approach

❏ Instructor says: "Cleared for GPS 17 Approach, missed approach instructions are hold as published at 4,500."

❏ Does pilot descend properly?
❏ Does pilot listen to AWOS?
❏ Does pilot slow to approach speed and maintain aircraft control?
❏ Does pilot conduct the approach properly?
❏ Does pilot allow autopilot to fly approach?
❏ Does pilot know when to turn off autopilot?
❏ On the missed approach, does pilot immediately power up? Immediate attitude change?
❏ Button-ology for the missed approach?

Continued

Hold at TEYOS

- ❏ Does pilot properly enter hold at assigned altitude?
- ❏ Does pilot ask for an EFC time if one isn't given?
- ❏ Does pilot report established in the hold?
- ❏ Does pilot correct for wind?
- ❏ After 2x in hold, on the outbound Instructor says: "Load the K24 GPS 35 with TEYOS as IAF."

GPS 35 Approach

- ❏ Over TEYOS, Instructor says: "Cleared GPS runway 35 approach. Circle to land Runway 17."
- ❏ Does pilot transition properly from hold to approach?
- ❏ Does pilot conduct the approach properly?
- ❏ Does pilot allow autopilot to fly approach?
- ❏ Does pilot know when to turn off auto?

Circle

- ❏ Does pilot use lowest circling minimums?
- ❏ Does the pilot circle close?
- ❏ Does the pilot descend below minimums from an appropriate position?

Landing

- ❏ Does the pilot perform prelanding checklist?
- ❏ Does the pilot use crosswind landing technique? On centerline? In first third of runway?
- ❏ After landing, did the pilot do nothing until off the runway and after full stop?
- ❏ Does the pilot shut down using checklists?

Return to LEX

- ❏ Does pilot transition smoothly through practice maneuvers?
    - ❏ Climbs at VX/VY and descents
    - ❏ Steep turns
    - ❏ Stalls: Power on and off, with and without flaps
    - ❏ Emergency descent
    - ❏ Which instrument approach was conducted at KLEX?
    - ❏ Does the pilot handle all radio communications to negotiate with ATC during approach?
- ❏ Does the pilot perform prelanding checklist?
- ❏ Does the pilot use crosswind landing technique? On centerline? In first third of runway?
- ❏ After landing, did the pilot do nothing until off the runway and after full stop?
    - ❏ Does the pilot shut down using checklists?

Have the pilot explain the scenario activity and the underlying concepts, principals and procedures within the scenario as a self-debrief.

Overall, did the pilot:

- ❏ Have a plan in mind before flight to handle each aspect of the flight with special consideration given to managing cockpit resources and maintain situational awareness?
- ❏ Make appropriate decisions during the flight?
- ❏ Use his technology?
- ❏ Prioritize cockpit tasks?
- ❏ Remain in control and in command?
- ❏ Have knowledge of and be able to execute the procedures correctly?
- ❏ Demonstrate good skills and awareness to avoid controlled flight into terrain?

Record additional notes on back. File in Pilot's Training Record.

DNY.BDR1 Scenario

Void Time Clearance, VOR Holds and a STAR

Objective: The purpose of this scenario is to provide practice at takeoff from uncontrolled field, navigate a STAR, while practicing VOR holds.

Preflight Discussion

Fully brief each element of the scenario:

- How to take off IFR from uncontrolled field—void time clearance
- How to read STARS
- Preview Bridgeport Connecticut, BRIDGEPORT ONE ARRIVAL, with emphasis on how to set up navaids to identify fixes
- Holding at intersection
- Holding at VOR station
- Hold Entries

Content

This scenario includes a STAR of about 55 NM (30 minutes), with 3 holds. Two racetracks per HOLD adds 24 minutes to the scenario time. Total flight time is about 79 minutes. Depending on the pilot's background, the scenario may end with a visual approach to a full stop or a VOR 24 approach to full stop.

Sim Set Up

- Broken clouds at 2,000 MSL with tops at 7,000 MSL, 10 miles visibility, winds at 6,000 MSL from 200 degrees, 25 kts. Winds at destination 210 degrees at 15 G 18.
- The scenario begins with a VFR takeoff from Kingston-Ulster, NY (20N). The pilot should contact BUF FSS via telephone for IFR clearance.
- The instructor must issue ATC clearances with proper phraseology and with an official-sounding voice and tone.
- Instructor: Make notes on this outline for pilot debriefing.

Scenario DNY.BDR1   Instructor Script and Evaluation Outline (2 pages)

Pilot's Name	Date / /

Before Start

❑ Kingston Airport Current Meteorological Conditions: time 0000Z (use local time). Wind 24020. Visibility 7, rain, ceiling 2000 overcast. Temperature 32/ dewpoint 31, altimeter 29.92.

FSS briefer says: "ATC clears Cessna 7261X to Bridgeport. Direct TRESA, Bridgeport One. Maintain 6,000. Squawk 1212. Upon entering controlled airspace contact New York Approach on 132.75. Void if not off by xxxx, time now xxxx."

Engine Start

❑ Does pilot perform checklists?

❑ Was takeoff time recorded?

❑ Does pilot establish on course V433 west of TRESA?

❑ Does pilot contact New York Approach after passing 1,300 MSL? (Don't answer until above 1,300 MSL)

❑ NY Approach says: "Cessna 7261X, squawk ident."

❑ NY Approach says: "Cessna 7261X radar contact. Climb to 6,000. Expect Bridgeport One, HOLD at SW TRESA, 6,000, SW, 1 minute right turns, expect further clearance at xxxx, time now xxxx."

❑ Does pilot correctly identify TRESA?

❑ Does the pilot correctly time crossing the fix?

❑ Does the pilot report established in the hold?

❑ Does the pilot anticipate wind and make appropriate correction?

❑ Does the pilot hold in the correct protected airspace?

❑ Does pilot time correctly?

Cruise

❑ After crossing TRESA in hold, NY approach says, "Cessna 61X, depart TRESA , 6,000, report PAWLING."

❑ NY Approach says: "Cessna 7261X, HOLD, 6,000, at PAWLINGS, on the 352 degree radial, 1 minute right turns, expect further clearance at xxxx, time now xxxx."

❑ Does pilot set up navaids correctly for hold?

❑ Does the pilot anticipate wind and make appropriate correction?

❑ Does the pilot hold in the correct protected airspace?

❑ Does pilot time correctly?

Holding

❑ NY Approach says, "Cessna 61X, 6,000, depart PAWLING report LOVES."

❑ After PAWLING, NY Approach says, "Cessna 61X, hold at LOVES as published, 6,000, 4 mile legs, expect approach clearance at xxxx, time now xxxx."

❑ Does pilot set up navaids correctly for hold?

❑ Does the pilot anticipate wind and make appropriate correction?

❑ Does the pilot hold in the correct protected airspace?

❑ Does pilot time correctly?

Approach

❑ During hold at LOVES, NY Approach says: "Cessna 61X, descend to 3,000. Report level at 3."

❑ NY Approach says: "Cessna 61X, confirm you have Information Sierra."

Continued next page

❑ Does pilot change frequency to 119.15 to get ATIS?	

❑ ATIS says: "Bridgeport Sikorsky Airport, Information Sierra, time 0000Z (use actual time) Wind 21015G18. Visibility 3, rain, ceiling 1200 broken. Temperature 32/ dewpoint 30, altimeter 29.92. VOR Runway 24 in use. Landing and departing Runway 29. Low level wind shear reported. Read back all runway crossing and hold short instructions. Advise on initial contact you have information Sierra."

❑ NY Approach says: "Cessna 61X, depart LOVES, 3,000, report DENNA."

❑ Does pilot report DENNA?

❑ After pilot reports DENNA, NY Approach says: "Cessna 7261X, Contact tower now 120.9. Good day."

❑ Does pilot contact tower correctly?

If pilot is a new instrument pilot, not yet trained in approaches:	If pilot is a rated instrument pilot and is able VOR Approach:
❑ Bridgeport Tower says, "Cessna 7261X, expect visual approach, windshear reported on final, ±10 knots, cleared to land runway 24 hold short Bravo."	❑ Tower says, "Cessna 7261X, cleared VOR 24 approach, report KNELL."
	❑ Over KNELL, Tower says, "61X Roger, windshear reported on final, ±10 knots, cleared to land runway 24 hold short Bravo.

Landing	
❑ Does the pilot complete prelanding checklist?	❑ Does pilot complete approach correctly?
❑ Was the pilot's descent path successful?	
❑ Does the pilot recognize displaced threshold?	
❑ Normal Landing Procedures	
❑ After Landing Procedures	

In general:

❑ Did the pilot understand the VOID clearance?
❑ Was the pilot able to "keep up" with the STAR? Did he get lost?
❑ Was the pilot thinking ahead to set up navaids correctly?
❑ Did the pilot keep control of his flight situation?
❑ Did the pilot use the autopilot to reduce workload?
❑ Were the holds legal?
❑ Record additional notes.

Record additional notes on back. File in Pilot's Training Record

Opportunity 2 Scenario
Gallatin to Bowling Green

Give this page to the pilot.

Objective: To give you the opportunity to practice decision-making skills while dealing with routine but unexpected events. Performance from this session is used to determine the extent that a decision-making process may need to be introduced by the instructor. It also provides a baseline for assessing improvement attributable to subsequent training.

- The instructor should have already briefed you on the concepts and objectives of Scenario Based Training.
- Carefully review your charts and mentally prepare as you would on a real-world flight.
- Ask questions before getting into the simulator.
- The scenario is a night, cross-country from Gallatin, TN (M33) to Bowling Green (KBWG) KY.
- Your alternate is Nashville, TN (KBNA).
- Contact BNA FSS on 122.55 for clearance.
- Weather is not a factor (not a source for situation or concern) in this scenario.
- You are authorized to use the autopilot and all cockpit resources.
- No instruction will be conducted once the scenario begins.
- All attempts to communicate with the "instructor" will go unnoticed.
- The session will last about 60 minutes.

You will need (available from the instructor if you don't have):

- L chart IFR and SE1 KY IAP.
- Any personal flying equipment you want in your cockpit.

Flight Plan

IFR	Number N45123	Type: PA32 /D	TAS 140	Departure KM33	Departure Time 0000	Altitude 5,000
Route: V49						
Destination: KBWG	Time in Route: 30					
Fuel on Board 5+30	Alternate: KBNA	Pilot Name and contact: Mr. Big, LEX 1.800.XXX.XXXX			# On Board: 1	
Aircraft colors: Red/White/Blue						

Current TAF M33	200/15G18KT OVC020 2SM-SHRA
Current TAF KBGW	180/15G18KT OVC020 2SM-SHRA
Current TAF KBNA	180/15G18 KT OVC020 2SM-SHRA

Clearance: ATC clears Saratoga 45123 to Bowling Green as filed. Climb and maintain seven thousand. Upon entering controlled airspace contact Memphis Center on 132.1, squawk 7227. Void if not off by (+10 minutes).

Get into the role, play the game and have fun. This is high-level training. Expect to make errors in your decision-making and expect to learn from the experience. Tailwinds and safe landing.

Opportunity 2   For Gallatin to Bowling Green, KY

Instructor's Eyes Only

Objective: To give the pilot an opportunity to practice decision-making skills while dealing with routine but unexpected events. The mission is a night IFR cross-country from Gallatin (KM33) to Bowling Green (KBGW). Alternate is Nashville (BNA). The flight navigates along Victor Airways. You depart with full fuel. Your mission begins with the pilot informing you of his choice in departure runway. Weather is not a factor for situation or concern. Encourage the pilot to use the autopilot and all other cockpit resources.

Key elements:

- Void time clearance from FSS.
- Departure M33 Runway 35 with procedure.
- Proper position report.
- HOLD.
- Amended clearance, Cruise.
- BWG VOR/DME 21 approach.
- Missed approach in low, night, IMC.
- ILS approach to minimums with wind shear.
- Crosswind landing.

Get into the role. Mentally rehearse the script. Set up the sim. The effectiveness of the scenario depends on your ability to simulate a "real" flight and the pilot's real reactions. No instruction is to be conducted once the scenario begins. Carefully monitor the pilot performance, aircraft control, and compliance with clearances/procedures and his decisions. Make notes. Your notes are to be filed in the training record.

Pilot will need:

- L chart, SE1 KY/TN IAP, pilot's scenario write-up, lap board, plus anything else the pilot wishes.

Instructor will need:

- L chart, SE1 KY/TN IAP, Script and Evaluation Outline, pencil/pen

The role of the instructor

1. Set up the simulator.
2. Have charts and script in the instruction station.
3. When pilot contacts ATC, lead him into choices that control the success of the scenario.
4. Offer no assistance as an instructor.

5. You ARE ATC. Use a formal and appropriate terminology when communicating.
6. You ARE ATIS/AWOS/ASOS. Use a formal voice when reading script.
7. Check off candidate actions and make notes for debriefing.

Simulator Set-Up

Note: The weather used to set up the sim is different than the weather given to the pilot.

Departure: Gallatin, TN (M33) Airport. Time: 9:30 PM local

Condition of runways: Light rain showers

Weather: M33 200/15 G18. Visibility 2 mist, 2,000 OVC. 32C/30C
   Winds en route at 3,000 = 050/20
   Tops 4000
   KBWG 180/15G18 2 mist, 1600 (MSL)
   OVC 32C/30C (slightly below VOR minimums)

Windshear set up:
   BWG +300 AGL winds 050/20
   KBNA (alternate airport) 180/15G18 2 mist, 6,160 OVC

Opportunity 2 Scenario   Instructor Script and Evaluation outline (2 pages)

Pilot's Name		Date / /
Engine Start		
❏ Does the pilot perform checklists?		
❏ Does the pilot contact Nashville Flight Service on 122.55 for clearance?		
❏ Nashville Flight Service Says: "ATC Clears Saratoga 45123 to Bowling Green as filed. Climb and maintain 5000. Upon entering controlled airspace contact Nashville Approach on 128.45, squawk 7227. Void if not off by (+10 minutes)."		
❏ Does pilot announce takeoff on UNICOM?		
❏ Was takeoff time recorded?		
❏ Which runway did pilot choose to takeoff from? 35 17		
❏ Does pilot need to comply with Departure Procedure on 35?		
(climb of 320 feet per NM to 1,000 (about 500 FPM at 90/100 kts ground speed)		
❏ When pilot contacts Nashville Approach, Nashville says: "Saratoga 123 Roger. Fly heading 270, Climb to five thousand, I won't pick you up on radar until you get higher. Report TANDS."		
❏ Does pilot correctly intercept airway promptly? Nashville Says, "Saratoga 123 radar contact, Contact Memphis Center now 133.85, good evening, sir."		
Cruise		
❏ Candidate establishes on-course, before TANDS and establishes cruise altitude?		
❏ Does he identify TANDS and make proper position report with correct format?		
❏ Over TANDS Memphis says, "Saratoga 123, V49, cleared to Bowling Green. Cruise five thousand."		
Approach		
❏ Does pilot recognize and comply with cruise clearance?		
❏ Does pilot plan descent early and report leaving altitude(s)?		
❏ When pilot reports leaving altitude, Memphis says: "Roger, report IFR cancellation this frequency or if unable this frequency, on the ground with FSS."		
❏ ASOS says: "Bowling Green Airport Automated Weather. Time 0000Z (use local time) Wind 18015G18. Visibility 2, mist, sky condition 2000 OVC. Temperature 32 C/dewpoint 30, altimeter is 2912."		
❏ Does pilot obtain ASOS?		
❏ Does pilot establish on the procedure before descent from cruise altitude?		
❏ What approach does pilot choose? ILS 3 NDB 3 VOR 3 VOR/DME 21		
❏ Does pilot execute approach correctly?		
❏ How did pilot conduct course reversal?		
❏ Does the pilot turn on PCL?		
❏ Does pilot announce intentions on CTAF?		
❏ Does pilot conduct prelanding checklist?		
❏ Does pilot comply with MDA and recognize missed approach condition?		
Missed Approach		
❏ Does pilot report missed approach?		
❏ After pilot reports missed, Memphis says: "Roger, sir, say intentions."		

Continued next page

❏ Does pilot have a plan? And transition easily?

❏ When pilot says his intentions, Memphis says,
  ❏ ILS Rwy 3? – "Climb to two thousand five hundred, direct NOORA, cleared ILS Runway 3, Cancel IFR on this frequency or if unable this frequency, on the ground with FSS. Frequency change approved."
  ❏ BNA? – "Roger Saratoga 123, Climb to four thousand, cleared to Nashville, intercept V49, Bowling Green altimeter 29.12. Sir, Nashville weather is beginning to come down; we are now overcast at eight hundred feet with 1 mile in rain. It seems to be coming down. Confirm you still wish Nashville?"

❏ Second approach procedure done correctly?
Landing
❏ Normal Landing Procedures
❏ After Landing Procedures
❏ Does pilot recognize and handle windshear correctly?
Overall: ❏ Was pilot prepared for the flight before entering sim, considering the information he was given? ❏ Did pilot consider all available approaches when choosing initial approach at BWG? ❏ Did pilot consider ILS 3 before announcing decision to deviate to alternate airport? ❏ Did the pilot choose to land downwind or circle? ❏ Did pilot think ahead and stay ahead of the flight? ❏ Was the pilot able to complete the flight? Did the pilot feel challenged? Record additional notes on back. File in Pilot's Training Record.

Chapter 6

Scenarios for Advanced Training

Advanced Maintenance

Flight Reviews, instrument proficiency checks (IPCs), and aircraft checkouts are to the pilot what inspections, modifications and upgrades are to the airplane. Strange, but most pilots invest more in preventative maintenance on the aircraft they fly than they do on themselves. Most pilots don't want an extensive flight review only because they don't see value in rehashing the same old maneuvers, time and time again. Yet allowing a pilot to squeak by with a minimal review every 24 months would be considered "failure mode" on an airplane.

Advanced training scenarios challenge the instructor to add value and challenge to what may be an experienced pilot's cockpit. The Flight Review, the IPC, and the aircraft checkout are three areas where an already-rated pilot may employ an instructor to have skills appraised or revalidated.

Flight Review Scenarios

Most pilots engaging in a Flight Review fall into either a rigid FAA checkride experience, or a nearly nothing, quick flight around the traffic pattern. An effective flight review should foster dialogue and open communications between pilot and instructor. It should not be a checkride experience; rather, it should be a fun, high-level training session to renew basic skills. It should include scenarios to validate good pilot judgment.

The scenario-based flight review must satisfy the requirements of 14 CFR 61.56, "Flight Review." If the pilot is instrument-rated, instrument procedures must be included to demonstrate the "safe exercise of the privileges of the pilot certificate" (14 CFR 61.56(a)(2)). However, before an IPC (§61.57(d)) is earned, the complete list of required procedures must be completed such as in the IPC scenarios starting on Page 96.

The scenarios below offer examples of a Flight Review based on the currency of the pilot.

Flight Review

Pilot flies regularly in flight review airplane and is presently current to fly as PIC.

Pre-appointment homework:

1. **www.faasafety.gov** Flight Review free online training course.
2. If instrument-rated, **www.asf.org** free online courses: "The IFR Adventure: Rules to Live By."
3. You and friends have tickets to opening night of a renowned play in St. Louis, MO. Plan a cross-country from KLEX to KSTL, complete with Navlog and actual DUATS weather briefing. The cross-country will begin during day, but end after dark. Your weight-and-balance includes you, your date, your best friend and his wife, plus fuel, and a total of 50 pounds luggage. Calculate takeoff and landing distances based on actual conditions.

Dual Ground Briefing: Judgment Risk Scenario Database and if instrument-rated, IFR Risk Scenarios. Review of assigned homework. Answer pilot's questions.

Flight (approximately 1.5 hours): Depart KLEX, using all cockpit equipment while en route to STL. An unexpected passenger illness requires a diversion to an alternate, ending with a short-field landing. After a short-field takeoff, perform power-off and power-on stalls and steep turns en route back to KLEX without the use of GPS or autopilot. Pilot maintains situational awareness and remains clear of LOU Charlie airspace. Divert to KDVK, for a soft-field landing, with an unexpected go-around. After dark, request an IFR approach into KDVK, if instrument rated. Practice required maneuvers from KDVK to KLEX. Include 2 landings to full stop after dark. Pilot handles all radio communications and other aspects of the flight as the sole pilot on board.

Flight Review

Pilot has not flown in previous year or more. Pilot is presently not current to fly as VFR PIC.

At the appointment time, pilot and instructor should agree that the flight review will comprise of at least one hour flight, plus one hour of ground training for each 12 months the pilot has not flown regularly.

Pre-appointment homework:

1. Open Book POH Exam.
2. www.faasafety.gov Flight Review free online training course.
3. Review assigned NTSB accidents.
4. You and friends are planning a beach-front vacation in Panama City, FL. Plan a cross-country from KLEX to KPFN, complete with Navlog and actual DUATS weather briefing. The cross-country will begin during day, but end after dark. It is a daytime departure but the flight will land after dark. Your weight and balance includes you, your date, your best friend and his wife, plus fuel, and a total of 50 lbs luggage. Calculate takeoff and landing distances based on actual conditions.

Dual Ground Briefing #1: Review assigned homework. Introduction to single-pilot resource management concepts. Highlight aircraft systems and operating procedures. Detailed preflight inspection followed by a few minutes in the cockpit to review aircraft equipment.

Flight #1: (approximately 1.3 hours) Depart KLEX, using all cockpit equipment while enroute to KPFN. An unexpected mechanical situation requires a diversion to an alternate, ending with a short-field landing. After a soft-field takeoff, returning in the direction of KLEX, practice stalls, steep turns, slow flight, a go-around and takeoffs and landings.

Homework:

1. Let's go shopping at Sporty's! Plan a cross-country from KLEX to Sporty's Pilot Shop (I69). On the way home, you'll make a stop at Falmouth, KY (I62) to pick up two friends. Complete a Navlog with DUATS weather briefing. The flight will depart LEX during day and land at I69 after dark. Plan the weight and balance to include your wife, and to pick up your best friend and his wife and fuel for the flight, plus 50 pounds of luggage. You purchase 50 pounds of goodies at Sporty's. Calculate takeoff and landing distance based on actual conditions.

Dual Ground Briefing #2: Review homework (weight and balance should be out of limits and will need to be adjusted). Judgment Risk Scenario Database

Flight #2: Fly the cross-country, approx 2.0 hours: Depart KLEX and use all cockpit equipment while en route to Sporty's (I69) with a hold and an IAP, if instrument rated, and a short-field landing. Take a break. After a short-field takeoff, proceed to I62 without the use of GPS or autopilot. Perform an IAP. Have the pilot maintain situational awareness and remain clear of CVG Bravo airspace to I62. Returning to KLEX after dark, divert to K27, for a soft field landing, with an unexpected go-around. Request an IFR approach into KLEX. Include a total of 3 landings to a full stop at night.

Additional ground and flights will be scheduled as necessary.

These Flight Review scenarios refresh the pilot's aeronautical knowledge by bringing it into use in the cockpit. His basic proficiency is renewed with practice in maneuvers. Additionally, the practical skills are made current with cross-country elements. Finally, the pilot's decision making and risk management skills are verified by the use of ground and flight scenarios in both day and night flight conditions.

Instrument Proficiency Check

Most instrument-training programs leave the pilot unequipped to deal with the real-world IFR environment. For some pilots, an Instrument Proficiency Check (IPC)* given by a seasoned instrument instructor is the first exposure to putting a whole flight together in actual conditions.

The conditions when an IPC is required are established in 14 CFR 61.57(e)(2). However, the structure of the IPC is found in the Instrument Rating Practical Test Standards (PTS).

While the maneuvers to be included and the conduct of the Flight Review are at the discretion of the instructor, the maneuvers, procedures and conduct of the IPC are dictated by the Practical Test Standards. The instructor is required to adhere to the standards and procedures contained in the PTS (see Table 6-1). According to the PTS, "The person giving the check should develop scenarios to assess the pilot's ADM and risk management skills during the IPC."

Instructors are to test the pilot's "correlative abilities rather than mere rote enumeration of facts." The instructor must evaluate the pilot's ability to use good aeronautical decision skills. In accomplishing this requirement, the instructor is to develop scenarios that "incorporate as many Tasks as possible to evaluate the pilot's risk management."

---

*(Note: The Instrument Proficiency Check used to be known as an Instrument Competency Check or ICC.)

Table 6-1. IPC from the PTS

Instrument Proficiency Check Required Tasks		
PTS Area of Operation	TASKS	
I Preflight Preparation	None	None required
II Preflight Procedures	None	None required
III Air traffic Control Clearances and Procedures	C	Holding Procedures
IV Flight by Reference to Instruments	B	Recovery from Unusual Flight Attitudes
V Navigation Systems	All	Intercepting and Tracking Navigational Systems and Arcs
VI Instrument Approach Procedures	All	A. Non-precision Approach. At least two approaches using two different types of navigational aids. One must include a procedure turn. One must be flown without the use of autopilot or radar vectors. Both are flown to the MAP. If the aircraft has an "operable and properly installed GPS, the applicant must demonstrate GPS approach proficiency" (PTS p. 8). B. Precision Approach (Flown to the DH) C. Missed Approach D. Circling Approach E. Landing from a Straight-In or Circling Approach
VII Emergency Operations	B, C, D	B. MEL Only – One Engine Inop During Straight and Level Flight and Turns C. MEL Only – One Engine Inop Approach D. Approach with Loss of Primary Flight Instrument Indicators
VIII Postflight Procedures	All	Checking Instruments and Equipment
Source: Adapted from FAA Instrument Rating Practical Test Standards for Airplane, Helicopter and Powered Lift, Page 16		

To demonstrate single-pilot competence, the instructor "will not assist the pilot in the management of the aircraft, radio communications, navigational equipment, and navigational charts."

The scenarios starting on the next page offer examples of IPCs based on the currency of the pilot.

Scenario: IPC in Airplane

Pre-appointment Homework:

1. **www.faasafety.gov** Flight Review free online training course.
2. **www.asf.org** free online courses: "The IFR Adventure: Rules to Live By."
3. Plan IFR cross-country (either IMC, or if VMC, then at night) from KLEX to KLOU with Navlog and complete DUATS weather briefing.

Dual Ground Briefing: IFR Risk Scenarios. IFR Regulation PowerPoint Scenario. Review of assigned homework. Answer pilot's questions.

Flight (approximately 1.5 hours): Your daughter is a singer scheduled to perform in two cities today: In Bardstown she opens the season's My Ole Kentucky Home, then in Danville, she sings the National Anthem at the football game. The only way to accomplish both dates is for you to fly her there. Depart KLEX, using all cockpit equipment while en route, fly direct to Bardstown (KBRY) and conduct the nonprecision approach and published missed approach. After holding, manually fly the airplane to Danville (KDVK). Conduct the GPS-A approach and circle to land for a short-field landing. Stop and take a break if you need. Perform a short-field takeoff. Returning to LEX you choose how to use the cockpit technology. At Lexington you'll complete the ILS to a full stop. You can expect routine but unexpected equipment failures and emergencies that you will be expected to handle. You will handle all radio communications and other aspects of the flight as the sole pilot on board.

Scenario: Extended IPC

For a pilot who has not flown instruments in more than 24 months, using a combination of FTD and airplane.

Pre-appointment Homework:

1. www.faasafety.gov Flight Review free online training course.
2. www.asf.org free online courses: "The IFR Adventure: Rules to Live By."
3. Plan IFR night cross-country from KBJC to KASE, one-way.

Dual Ground Briefing: IFR Risk Scenarios. IFR Regulation PowerPoint Scenario. Review of assigned homework. Answer pilot's questions.

ATD Flight (approximately 1.5 hours): First Look Scenario—Denver, Jeffco Airport (BJC) to Aspen (ASE) Airport, LOC/DME E approach to full stop.

Plan IFR cross-country: (prefer IMC, or if VMC, at night) from KLEX V297 to KLOZ Direct to KSME and return.

Night flight (approx 2.0 hours): Using all cockpit technology and autopilot, depart KLEX navigating along Victor airways to KSME, full procedure turn, ILS RWY 6 LOZ, missed approach with published VOR climbing-hold to 4,000 MSL. Direct to KSME, LOC RWY 5. Published NDB hold ending with a short-field landing. Take a break. After a short field takeoff, perform power-off stalls and steep turns enroute back in the direction of KLEX, without the use of GPS or autopilot. VOR-A approach at KLEX with circle to short-field landing on active runway. You will handle all radio communications and as much of the flight as practical as the sole pilot on board.

Homework: Plan IFR cross-country (prefer IMC, or if VMC, at night) from KLEX, Direct to K24, Direct to KDVK, and return with Navlog and complete DUATS weather briefing.

Day flight (approximately 2.0 hours): Using all cockpit technology and autopilot, depart KLEX GPS direct to K24, where you will perform the GPS approach to the active runway followed by the published missed approach. After a hold, continue direct to KDVK. Perform the full procedure turn NDB-A with a circle to land and a soft-field landing. Take a break. With a void time clearance from FSS, perform a soft-field takeoff, and head in the direction of KLEX. While en route to KLEX you will handle routine but unexpected situations including unusual attitudes and emergency operations. When ready, request radar vectors to the GPS approach to the active runway with a short-field landing. You will handle all radio communications and each aspect of the flight as the sole pilot on board.

Although the basic IPC syllabus has been dictated, the CFI should continue to consider the needs of the pilot for each lesson plan. There should be mutual agreement on where additional training may be needed.

The most common problem with rusty pilots "is pilot workload, aggravated by the need for multi-tasking. A single IFR pilot also serves as navigator, radio operator, systems manager, onboard meteorologist, record keeper, and sometimes, flight attendant. En route flights in benign weather are usually not too stressful, but add high-density traffic in poor weather conditions or a significant equipment malfunction, and overload may not be far away."[1]

An aviation training device is an excellent training platform for the IPC. Still, there has not been a general ATD approved by the FAA National Simulation Program to perform the circling approach maneuver as described in the Instrument Rating PTS. Therefore, the IPC cannot be performed completely in a training device.

Aircraft Checkouts

Aircraft checkouts at most flight schools involve minimal ground evaluation and about an hour of maneuvers. There is usually no evaluation of the pilot's judgment skills or an assessment of his ability to handle routine decisions pertaining to airport operations, airspace, terrain or aircraft installed equipment failures. Aircraft checkouts are an opportunity to use ground and flight scenarios to evaluate the prospective rental pilot.

Aircraft Checkout Scenario 1

Previous experience in the make and model, but new to the flight school.

Pre-appointment homework, to be reviewed and adjusted prior to the flight: (The weight and balance condition should be beyond limits.) Cross-country from KLEX to KBRY: Cross-country Navlog. Weather briefing. Aircraft weight and balance for the pilot, wife, best friend and his wife, plus fuel for the flight, plus 50 pounds of luggage. Calculated takeoff distance based on the conditions.

Dual Ground Preflight Briefing: Judgment Risk Scenario Database

Flight, approximately 1.5 hours: Depart KLEX and use all cockpit equipment while enroute direct to Bardstown (KBRY) with a short-field landing. After a short field takeoff, perform power-off and power-on stalls and steep turns enroute back to KLEX without the use of GPS or autopilot. Have the pilot maintain situational awareness and remain clear of LOU Charlie airspace. Divert to KDVK, for a soft field landing, with an unexpected go-around. Request an IFR approach into KDVK, if instrument-rated.

Aircraft Checkout Scenario 2

No previous experience in make and model.

Pre-appointment homework: Open Book POH Exam.

Dual Ground Preflight Briefing #1: Review POH Exam. Review NTSB accidents. Introduction to single-pilot resource management concepts. Highlight aircraft systems and operating procedures. Detailed preflight inspection followed by a few minutes in the cockpit to introduce installed equipment.

Flight #1: Departing in the direction of KFFT, practice stalls; steep turns, takeoffs and landings, an IFR approach (if instrument rated), a go around and a landing to a full stop. Take a break. Returning to KLEX, use cockpit technology on an instrument approach.

Homework: Plan a cross-country from KLEX to Sporty's Pilot Shop (I69), to Falmouth, KY (I62). This flight will depart during day and end after night. Cross-country Navlog. Weather briefing. Aircraft weight and balance for the pilot, wife, best friend and his wife, plus fuel for the flight, plus 50 pounds of luggage. Calculated takeoff distance based on the conditions.

Dual Ground Preflight Briefing #2: Review homework (weight and balance should be out of limits and will need to be adjusted). Judgment Risk Scenario Database

Flight #2: Fly the cross-country, approx 2.0 hours: Depart KLEX and use all cockpit equipment while en route to Sporty's (I69) with a hold and an IAP, if instrument rated, and a short-field landing. Take a break. After a short-field takeoff, proceed to I62 without the use of GPS or autopilot. Perform an IAP. Have the pilot maintain situational awareness and remain clear of CVG Bravo airspace to I62. Returning to KLEX, divert to K27, for a soft-field landing, with an unexpected go-around. Request an IFR approach into KLEX with a night landing.

An aircraft checkout of this type allows the instructor to evaluate the pilot's ability to control the airplane, exercise command as well as test his situational awareness and decision-making. Depending on the checkout aircraft, additional elements should also be included:

- All installed instruments and equipment should be incorporated into in-flight scenarios. Include such things as engine monitoring, datalink, speed-spoilers. On the ground include such items as emergency exits.ˇ
- A checkout in six-place aircraft should include one flight at gross weight. Flight characteristics are drastically different when an aircraft of this size is fully loaded.
- Pilots flying six-place aircraft should be asked to rehearse a passenger emergency evacuation drill with passengers during the checkout.
- If this is the pilot's first plane with more than 235 HP, takeoffs

and landing practice is important to instill centerline discipline and control.

- If the aircraft is turbocharged, the checkout should include a flight to altitude. Training should include powerplant temperature control, high-altitude physiology, descent planning and use of supplemental oxygen equipment.

Pilots previously trained in a maneuvers-oriented course will marvel at how difficult flying a scenario is. Not that the plane is any more difficult to control during a scenario, but the amount of headwork the pilot is expected to perform is probably more than what has been asked of the pilot in previous training.

Industry Update

Occasionally an instructor comes across a pilot who hasn't flown in a really long time. These pilots will find that much has changed while they were away. These pilots require a complete "industry update" to help them feel comfortable in the aviation that we know today. Some items include:

- Pilots who have not flown since September 11, 2001 will need an introduction to GA Flight School Awareness Security Training, NACO versus NOAA, online IFR instrument approach chart availability, preferred internet aviation resources, Wide Area Augmentation System (WAAS), Land and Hold Short Operations (LAHSO), and Temporary Flight Restrictions (TFRs).

- Pilots who last flew in the 1990s may need an introduction to the new kinder/gentler FAA, airspace classification, changes in weather reporting format, AWOS/ASOS, Aircraft Product Liability Reform, medical requirements, internet weather products, cell phone use (including FSS), runway incursion awareness including LAHSO/airport diagrams, NDB decommissioning and GPS.

Conclusions

Instructors engaged in scenario-based training often hear, "My head is about to explode!" from pilots—meaning that the pilot is thinking more than he is accustomed to. "Safe flight requires a pilot to continuously sniff out and compensate for changes in the flight from planned parameters."[2] Even accomplished and experienced pilots need to review knowledge, skills and judgment to stay proficient.

Don't assume that just because a pilot has a lot of hours or years in the cockpit, that he's not in need of a thorough review. Although there is redundancy in the aeronautical knowledge required for each pilot certificate, training to earn a new certificate does not improve retention. Studies show that much of what is learned for FAA test questions gets forgotten.[3] That's why it's so important that each flight review, instrument proficiency check and aircraft checkout include a review of knowledge areas. It's a good reason to keep the review practical too.

Exercises

1. You are a flight instructor with a tailwheel endorsement and 10 hours in an Aeronca Champ. A pilot would like you to give her a flight review in her Luscomb 8A. In exchange, she has agreed to allow you to use the airplane to fly where you want and build as many hours as you like. Research these two aircraft and their flight characteristics. What are the differences between the two aircraft that you should be aware of?

2. You are a new flight instructor and your pilot is a 20,000-hour retired airline captain in need of a flight review. Discuss how you may feel uncomfortable evaluating a very experienced pilot's skills and how to best deal with those issues.

3. You are a new instrument instructor with little actual instrument "cloud time." Describe how you will prepare yourself for the "real world" environment of conducting an instrument proficiency check in actual conditions. Consider what personal minimums you will use and how often will you re-evaluate your personal minimums. Does day versus night affect your minimums? If the weather is below your personal minimums, what words will you use to explain to your pilot that you won't fly today even though it's legal to do so? Write a paper to reflect on your thoughts.

4. You are a flight instructor asked to perform an aircraft checkout in an aircraft make and model you have never flown before. How will you prepare for your lesson? Now, consider that you are very comfortable in this make and model, but the aircraft has a GPS and avionics package that you have never flown with before. How will you prepare for your lesson? Lastly, consider that you are comfortable with this make and model and avionics package, but you find that the aircraft has a unique modification that drastically changes the takeoff and landing flight characteristics. How will you prepare for your lesson?

Chapter 7

Scenarios for Instructor Training

What is your definition of a good flight instructor? Certainly a good instructor must have aeronautical skill, human-relations skills and judgment. But a flight instructor's judgment extends beyond merely the decisions he makes during his flying. A flight instructor must have the ability to grow and nurture good judgment in other pilots.

CFI Candidates

This book teaches a series of examples of how to develop good judgment in pilots. These examples can also be used by instructors who are training CFI candidates. Scenarios provide a variety of practical tools suited to train CFI candidates. This material is for candidates who wish to become:

- Expert in technical knowledge
- More precise in aircraft control
- Good communicators
- Empathetic listeners
- Confident in a wide variety of situations
- Capable of avoiding instructional surprises
- Responsible aviation citizens

This chapter focuses on the scenarios used in training an initial flight instructor. Scenarios included here help the CFI candidate learn to speak in a professional manner, revise a lesson plan template from the Aviation Instructor's Handbook, and practice proper student supervision. A "Pilot Logbook Exercise" is included in order to challenge the candidate's understanding of the regulations, by designing a "finish up" training plan from a sample student "logbook." Also, a "Learning Plateau Game" affords instructors greater insight into the phenomenon of learning plateaus. Covered at the end are scenarios to help new instructors look beyond training to consider working conditions.

The best way to understand how to bring these elements together is to follow a CFI candidate's flight and ground training and the scenarios used in his instruction.

Talking

Begin the CFI candidate talking and teaching immediately. He's not ready to teach an aviation lesson plan, but he can make an effective presentation about assigned homework.

> *Teaching Mission:* Log online and visit www.nafinet.org. Become familiar with your professional organization. At "nafinet," learn about the Master Instructor program. Prepare a formal 15-minute talk, to present during a meeting of your peers to instruct them about NAFI and its benefits. Include information about the Master Instructor Program and how earning a Master CFI might benefit the aviation industry. Your presentation must be complete, logically organized and presented in a mature, professional manner. Make eye contact and use appropriate body language. Don't read from notes (although referencing notes is acceptable). Solicit and answer questions from your audience.

This lesson gets the candidate started on how to research resources, and then teaching others about what he's found. This type of initial teaching, whether one-on-one or in front of a class, allows the candidate to express himself, to develop human relation skills, and to think on his feet while answering questions. Other subjects of value that can be assigned for a candidate to teach might include the Nall Report at www.aopa.org, free online courses at www.asf.org, resources for instructors available at www.faasafety.gov, and aircraft incident reports available at www.asrs.gov.

Lesson Plan Template

Every instructor training program begins with writing lesson plans. Lesson plan examples have previously been shown in chapters of this book, but most CFI candidates will use one of the templates provided in the *Aviation Instructor's Handbook*.

Consideration of system safety should be included even in maneuver lesson plans. Revision of traditional lesson plan templates to include risk management, decision making, learner-centered grading and single pilot resource management is easy. The following list is an example of a lesson on stalls.

Objective

To familiarize the student with the stall warnings and handling characteristics of the airplane as it approaches a stall. To develop the student's skill in recognition and recovery from stalls. To promote the student's understanding of how stalls affect system safety. To promote the student's situational awareness, risk management and aeronautical decision making while practicing stalls.

Content:

- Configuration of airplane for power-on and power-off stalls.
- Observation of airplane attitude, stall warnings, and handling characteristics as it approaches a stall.
- Control of airplane attitude, altitude, and heading.
- Initiation of stall recovery procedures.
- Opportunities for student to make Aeronautical Decisions pertaining to stall entry and recognition of stalls.
- Managing the risks associated with stalls

Schedule:

- Preflight Discussion: 30
- Instructor Demonstration: 15
- The Scenario: Best Ability maneuvers review and Introduction to Stalls: 60
- Postflight Critique and Explanation of Homework: 30

Equipment:

- Instructor: Chalkboard or notebook for preflight discussion. Handout.
- Student: Paper for note taking

Instructor's actions:

- Review previously assigned homework.
- Preflight—Discuss scenario objective. Discuss managing the risk in stalls concerning controlled flight into terrain. Discuss opportunities to use cockpit technology during the lesson.
- Inflight — Demonstrate elements. Demonstrate power-on and power-off stalls and recovery procedures. Nurture student practice.
- Postflight—Allow student to critique performance. Evaluate the student's understanding of how this maneuver affects the Pilot, The Plane, The Environment, The Operation, and the Situation. Evaluate decision-making. Assign study material. Document training.

Student's actions:

- Preflight—Discuss scenario objective and resolve questions.
- Inflight—Perform the scenario using SRM. Explain and Practice each maneuver.
- Postflight—Participate in Learner-Centered Grading.

Completion Standards:

- Student should explain and perform "system safety." Student should demonstrate competency in controlling the airplane at airspeeds approaching a stall. Student should recognize and take prompt corrective action to recover from power-on and power-off stalls maintaining an awareness of the risks associated with controlled flight into terrain.

This lesson plan reminds the CFI candidate to include the safety system at each point in the lesson. It allows the instructor to present the maneuver as one element in the total safety system.

Teaching and Supervising

After the CFI candidate can properly speak as a professional and his lesson plans have been revised to include thinking skills, then it's time to begin teaching and supervising.

Instructors sometimes confuse teaching and supervising. If an instructor is talking, directing, showing or demonstrating to the pilot what to do, he is teaching. Teaching is the technique used at the start of each new skill and knowledge area. However, before the instructor is assured that the pilot has "got it" the instructor must supervise the pilot doing "it."

Supervising requires the instructor to get in the plane, not say anything, and not touch anything. A supervisor sits back and watches the pilot at work managing the task without input, prompting or direction. Any help from the instructor will possibly mask problem areas. For example, it's a common temptation for instructors to instinctively hold the toe brakes while the students goes through his start procedure. This may seem like a good back up step but it interferes with the student's learning pattern. After a period of proper supervision, then the evaluation can begin to correct the problem area.

Don't make the mistake of assuming that testing is an effective form of supervising. It's not. A pilot acts, flies and makes decisions differently when being tested. When on a test, pilots perform as though on a stage. Supervision is the act of observing pilot activities during routine operations, not when he's performing for a test.

Pilot training requires an instructor to alternate between the roles of teacher and supervisor. The instructor teaches new skills. Then he supervises the pilot's performance—both the elements of the task and the pilot's headwork in making decisions. It is likely the instructor will find himself teaching something again, after he discovers after supervising that the pilot doesn't "have it." It's during the supervision phase that the instructor is able to ascertain the pilot's level of learning.

Balancing teaching and supervising is an important aspect of an instructor's job. "Improper Student Supervision" is a term the NTSB uses on too many incident reports to explain an instructional flight gone wrong. It's an excellent reason for more scenarios.

Scenarios in Teaching

The best tool for teaching the CFI candidate is a personal tape recorder. Have the candidate "teach" into the recorder, then play it back and listen to himself. Teaching the tape recorder is better than teaching a friend—whether they are pilots or not. The candidate is able to listen to his recording and to evaluate himself. The tape recorder is the quickest way to rid the candidate of the "um's" and "ah's" that new instructors suffer from. The recorder also develops critical listening and evaluating skills. A Teaching Mission might look like this:

> *Teaching Mission:* Prepare a 20-minute preflight briefing to teach steep turns. Use as many attempts as you need and practice teaching into the tape recorder until you achieve the one "Best Ability" recording that you are pleased and proud to submit to the Chief Instructor for evaluation.

The best tool for teaching the CFI candidate is a personal tape recorder. Have the candidate record practice-teaching sessions. Later, the candidate and instructor are able to review the recording for effective evaluation. The tape recorder is the quickest way to rid the "hum's" and "ah's" that new instructors offer suffer with. The candidate can hear how to improve material organization and hear where additional information might be needed.

Scenarios in Supervising

The Aviation Instructor's Handbook dedicates only a short section on student supervision[1]; therefore many instructors gloss over this crucial skill. While a pilot trains for a checkride, the real test is what the pilot does during normal operations: without prompting, without assistance, and without a reason to "perform." How the pilot conducts a flight without prompting is what the instructor hopes to learn through proper supervision.

Supervising Preflight Inspection

The pilot previously demonstrated his ability to conduct the preflight inspection. A smart instructor stands back and supervises the pilot's inspection. The instructor stands about 10 feet away—within earshot in case he's needed, but far enough away to give the pilot space and time to perform the entire task without appearing to hover over him.

Good Supervisory Skills

Instructors who have developed good supervisory skills have the ability to get in the plane, sit down, not say anything, not touch anything, and not feel an overwhelming need to "help" unless the pilot asks or demonstrates that he needs it.

> The smart instructor directs the pilot to preflight, engine start, run-up and taxi to the runway. After supervising the preflight inspection, the instructor will get in the plane, buckle up and not say anything. He'll watch carefully all that the pilot does until the plane arrives at the runway hold short line. He offers, "You did a great job on the run-up checklist, but from now on let's stay on the centerline of the taxiway. Centerline discipline is important all the time, not just during takeoff."

Be Clear On the Role

The pilot should be aware of which tasks are being taught and which are being supervised. The instructor must be clear about if and when he expects to resume the teaching role.

> The smart instructor says, "We have been through the run-up checklist now a couple of times. Do you think you can do it yourself today without my help? Let's see you manage it. I will sit back and watch. You let me know when you're ready to contact ground control and I'll be ready to help you with communications."

As training progresses, reduce the time spent in leading and directing pilot activities. Increase the time spent supervising the pilot performing tasks. Look for the pilot's ability to perform consistently and without prompting or reminding. Of course, a smart instructor will correct any mistakes in technique and he will prompt or remind if necessary. Nevertheless, the goal is that the instructor be needed less as training progresses.

> Air Traffic Control radios, "Cessna 123, make short approach or extend downwind. Say intentions." The pilot, who is nearing first solo, engages his instructor with a quizzical look, hoping for a decision. The smart instructor shrugs his shoulders, "What would you do if I weren't here? You say what your intentions are."

Now the pilot knows that he should make decisions and control the aspects of the flight that he is qualified to control. After supervising the pilot's decision, the instructor knows more about what the pilot's reactions will be during solo flights. In addition, should the pilot make the wrong decision, the instructor is prepared to resume the teaching role—to assist, to keep the flight safe, and to instruct the pilot so that he handles things differently the next time.

Preventing Instructional Surprises

"Smart Instructor" doesn't allow surprises to happen during instruction. He reduces the chance that a bad situation may develop with proactive supervision. As a proactive supervisor, he mentally rehearses with the pilot before taking to the cockpit. By doing so, Smart Instructor knows how the pilot will react. There is less chance of surprises when both the instructor and pilot have agreed in advance what is to happen.

> Smart Instructor is preparing the pilot for arrival at the destination. At the table they talk, "Which runway are you planning to use? From our course, how will you enter the traffic pattern? What altitude will you use as traffic pattern altitude? When will you begin your descent from cruise to traffic pattern altitude? Where will you listen to ATIS? Who will you be talking to upon entering the traffic pattern? What are the differences between our operations at this airport and what we normally do at our home airport?"

The chance of instructional surprises is reduced when the pilot is mentally prepared in advance. It helps the pilot when the instructor doesn't have to intervene in the middle of a busy situation. It also reduces the amount of help the pilot might need, allowing the instructor to give only a nudge to keep the pilot moving on his own—without completely taking over the situation to resolve the problem for the pilot.

> Smart Instructor prepares the pilot for the flying in gusty winds. "The conditions are challenging today, so let's quickly review the concepts so they're fresh in your mind. Explain how you'll correct for wind drift on final with these winds? And if you get close to the ground and don't like what you see, what will you do? Tell me how you will flare with strong crosswinds. How might our flight operations today be different from what we normally do? When I say, 'I have the flight controls,' what will you do?"

The most uncomfortable aspect in the first hours of dual given for a new instructor is the uncertainty of what the pilot will do. Some new instructors hope to prevent surprises by being quick to grab the controls away from the pilot. Proactive supervision is better.

Preventing Surprises During Solo

Preventing surprises is also important on solo and solo cross-country. A systematic, mental rehearsal before the solo pilot takes to the cockpit benefits him with a "warm up" before takeoff. It also benefits the instructor with the security of knowing how the solo pilot will respond to in-flight situations. In the event that the instructor finds a deficiency in the pilot's plan during the warm-up, the instructor is there to offer input. Smart Instructor always reminds the pilot that a 180-degree turn to return home is an approved maneuver and at times, the best choice.

> Smart Instructor is supervising the pilot's Navlog planning for the first solo cross-country. They sit at the table to talk, "Tell me about the weather today. Where is the weather coming from? If you run into unexpected weather along this leg, what will you do? How will you navigate there? Is there any terrain or obstacles to be aware of en route there? What cockpit resources will help relieve the workload of an unexpected diversion? Do you have that airport tabbed in your AFD for easy access? At what point would you decide to simply turn around and return home? Now along this leg…"

Supervising by Solo Debriefing

The debriefing offers additional supervision opportunities for the instructor. By asking questions and having the pilot replay the solo flight, the instructor can see what valuable skills and knowledge the pilot practiced. It may read like a drill sergeant's interrogation, but with an easy conversational tone the instructor can learn exactly what happened in the cockpit during a solo cross-country.

> Smart Instructor is happy to see the pilot's timely return from a solo cross-country. They sit at the table to debrief, "Let's see your Navlog. Where is the takeoff time written down? Where did you open your flight plan? I don't see an ATA recorded next to this checkpoint…"

Supervising the Total Training Process

The total training process is often overlooked. Supervising the total training process provides continuity between training events. It ensures that nothing is forgotten. Make a plan for the week's activities. Keep the pilot abreast of where he is and what's coming next in the training process.

The pilot, the instructor, and the industry will feel the results of "inadequate student supervision." The pilot will not be a complete pilot, having achieved only a rote level education. The pilot will not feel completely comfortable and confident in flying, and may quickly leave aviation. The instructor cannot verify the pilot's skill or decision-making.

The instructor is not completely comfortable and confident in the pilot's abilities and hopes everything will be okay. The industry is at risk for incidents, accidents, damaged aircraft and injured people.

Pilot Logbook Exercise

The pilot logbook exercise challenges the CFI candidate to review a pilot's training documentation and ascertain the pilot's eligibility for the FAA practical exam. This practical exercise occurs every day at flight schools across the country. While a prudent instructor will review all areas with a student and will make one "catch all" endorsement, that is not an acceptable option for this exercise.

The CFI candidate is expected to review the logbook and make a detailed list of each item missing or in need correction to meet eligibility requirements. The exercise is a test of the CFI candidate's understanding of training regulations. This exercise should be completed open book with the FAA regulations as reference.

Logbook of John Q. Student—Private Pilot Candidate

Mr. John Q. Student has just walked into your flight school and presented his logbook for your review. He wants you to tell him what is required for him to complete private pilot training. Your mission is to review his logbook, making a "to-do" list required to meet the eligibility requirements for the Private Pilot Practical Exam.

Although we understand that you will conduct a complete review of all subject areas, the purpose of this lesson is to make sure that you understand the practical applications of regulatory requirements. Make an itemized "to-do" list based on regulatory requirements. Unless noted, all flights originate from airport KFFT.

Other Notes:

- Mr. Student is 20 years old and a U.S. citizen
- Medical Certificate: a second class, issued 20 months ago
- Student Pilot Certificate: endorsed for solo and solo cross-country in C-152.
- FAA Knowledge Exam Results: 74%, passed 23 months ago.

(See Table 7-1 on the next page.)

Table 7-1. Logbook of John Q. Student

Date = Today minus days	Make/ Model	Comments/Notes/Endorsement	X/C	Night	Hood	Dual	Solo
-102 days	C-172	Discovery Flight Red Baron, 1231234 CFI Exp 00/00				.5	
-95	C-152	Preflight, taxiing, S & level, turns. Red Baron, 1231234 CFI Exp 00/00				1.5	
-85	C-172	MCA, stalls, TO&L Red Baron, 1231234 CFI Exp 00/00				1.5	
-80	C-152	Review Red Baron, 1231234 CFI Exp 00/00				1.4	
-75	C-172	TAP, traffic patterns, TO&L Red Baron, 1231234 CFI Exp 00/00				1.4	
-70	C-172	TO&L, emergencies Red Baron, 1231234 CFI Exp 00/00				1.3	
-65	C-152	TO&L Red Baron, 1231234 CFI Exp 00/00				1.3	
-60	C-152	Normal and crosswind takeoff and landings Red Baron, 1231234 CFI Exp 00/00				1.5	
-55	C-152	TO&L Red Baron, 1231234 CFI Exp 00/00				1.5	
-50	C-172	Normal takeoffs and landings. 3 at controlled field Red Baron, 1231234 CFI Exp 00/00				1.3	
-45	C-152	TO&L, GAR, review Red Baron, 1231234 CFI Exp 00/00				1.2	
-40	C-152	TO&L Red Baron, 1231234 CFI Exp 00/00				1.0	.5
-35	C-172	Solo					1.5
-34	C-152	Solo					1.5
- 33	C-152	Night procedures Red Baron, 1231234 CFI Exp 00/00		2.5	.3	2.5	
-32	C-152	Night x/c – KLEX – 0I8 – KIOB – KLEX Red Baron, 1231234 CFI Exp 00/00	1.9	1.9		1.9	
-31	C-152	X/C KLEX – KDVK – I39 – KLEX Red Baron, 1231234 CFI Exp 00/00	2.8			2.8	
-30	C-152	Solo X/C – KLEX – KLOU – LEX	2.3				2.3
-25	C-152	Instrument, ASR Approach, Review Red Baron, 1231234 CFI Exp 00/00		1.0	1.1	1.0	

-20	C-152	Solo practice, TO&L					2.0
-19	C-152	Solo practice					2.0
-17	C-152	Solo practice					2.1
-15	C-172	Solo practice					2.5
-10	C-152	Practice review Red Baron, 1231234 CFI Exp 00/00			1.6	1.9	
The End							

One might assume this to be a straightforward exercise, as all requirements are clearly spelled out in the regulations. Still, instructors interpret regulations with creative flair.

Reviewing this scenario with a CFI candidate opens the door to consider the traditional abbreviations customarily recorded in pilot logbooks and how he will interpret them as evidence of regulatory requirements. "TO&L" and "MCA" are common abbreviations for takeoff and landings and minimum controllable airspeed. Lesser-known might be "TAP" for Turn Around a Point and "BAI" for Basic Attitude Instrument. Abbreviations can be problematic and fall on the judgment of the instructor in interpreting and evaluating if a pilot has met the training requirements.

Another interpretation may be the number of night takeoffs and landings. How many will Mr. Student be credited with? Flight -32 shows four destinations on the cross-country flight. Was a night landing made at each or only on the last? Were landings to a full stop?

The CFI candidate will decide how to interpret logbook errors such as the one recorded on flight -25. "1.1" was logged as hood while only "1.0" was logged as total. There is another error in Flight -50 where three TO&Ls at the controlled field were recorded, but not to a full stop.

Red Baron, the original instructor, allowed Mr. Student to solo without having met the 15 requirements of 14 CFR §61.87 and to solo cross-country without meeting each of the requirements of §61.93(c). Red Baron allowed the student to solo a C-172 while his student pilot certificate was endorsed for a C-152. Will our CFI candidate presume that because an experienced instructor allowed it, that he should too? How will our CFI candidate check the distances to unfamiliar cross-country destinations? Is the CFI candidate responsible to see that cross-countries meet the requirements of §61.109?

The complete to-do list to properly document Mr. Student's training will cost more time and money than it should have. The complete list of errors committed by Red Baron is lengthy. As a result, Mr. Student must be required to repeat portions of his training so that it will be documented correctly. Sadly, this scenario was constructed from a real logbook, from a real pilot who paid real money for his training. It opens the door for the CFI candidate to consider the long-term ramifications of messy paperwork not completed with thoughtfulness. These are the legal, ethical and professional issues on the business-side of flight instructing.

Learning Plateau Exercise

The learning plateau is often misunderstood, giving heartburn to pilots and instructors. Because it is so widely misunderstood instructors dismiss it, or through misunderstanding, may unknowingly even create it.

This "Learning Plateau Game" was discovered in the 1970s at a Flight Instructor Refresher Clinic. The game works best when conducted in small groups. The objective is to locate the number "1" and draw a circle around it. Then with the pencil still on the paper, draw a line to "2." Draw a circle around it. Find each successive number in sequence, as fast as possible, within the allotted time.

The game begins with each participant having a set of 10 copies of the game sheet shown in Figure 7-1, turned upside down on the table. The facilitator starts a stopwatch for 60 seconds. When the signal is given, each participant begins circling each sequential number. At the end of 60 seconds, the facilitator calls TIME. The participants stop and lay down the pencils. Each participant should plot their highest number on a graph. The facilitator polls the group for their highest number found and plots the average of the group on a group graph.

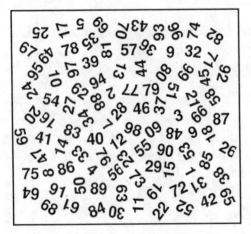

Figure 7-1. Learning Plateau game sheet.

Repeat the exercise. The facilitator calls out START, the participants turn over their paper and begin drawing to and circling each number in sequence. After the facilitator calls TIME, the results are graphed individually and as a group. The exercise is performed 10 times.

For anyone who doubted the existence of the learning plateau or for those under the impression that it didn't apply to them, it is a revelation. At about the third round, groans of frustration are heard as participants search in vain for the next number in sequence—the very same number that was easily found in the last round. At about round five, disbelief offsets frustration as reality presents itself: they have encountered the learning plateau.

The group graph will illustrate the classic example shown in the *Aviation Instructor's Handbook* (see Figure 7-2 below) although individual graphs will vary somewhat. Experience has shown males and females will graph differently (see Figures 7-3 and 7-4). If the group contains enough of both sexes, it is interesting for the group to witness the difference in the way the sexes "learn." Generally, female graphs have sharper angles with higher peaks and lower valleys, while male graphs are smoother, with smaller peaks and valleys.

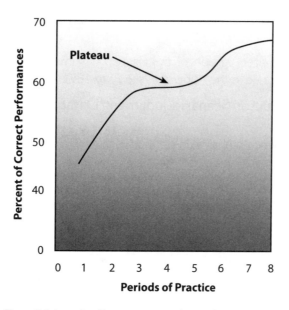

Figure 7-2. Learning Plateau game results graph.

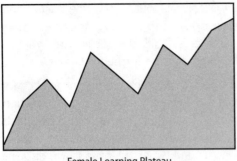

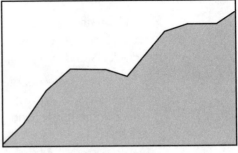

Female Learning Plateau   Male Learning Plateau

Figures 7-3 and 7-4. Typical female and male group results graph.

It is the simplest of exercises. It requires no learning and no technical facts to memorize. It documents that the human brain is what it is, and that our brains simply require time to digest information—even something as redundant as where the next number-in-sequence is.

Instructors learn from the exercise that requiring a pilot to repeat lessons does not yield better results or more proficiency. In fact, allowing a pilot to repeat any lesson more than three times starts him down the runway to a learning plateau. Better to move the pilot to another area of the curriculum and give that information a break than to suffer the frustrations of a learning plateau.

A full-page-sized version of the Figure 7-1 game sheet, suitable for training, is located in the Appendix (see Page 189).

Flight Instructor Scenario Judgment Database

Just as in pilot training, the Judgment Scenario Database offers a CFI candidate mental rehearsal in decision making for routine demands on the job (See Table 7-2). The database includes judgment practice for dealing with customers and dealing with flight training business issues.

Instructor Flight Training

After the technical information is mastered and the CFI candidate can teach effectively while on the ground, it's time to move into the cockpit. A flight instructor curriculum assumes that the candidate is proficient in performing maneuvers in the training airplane. The flight instructor curriculum is designed to teach supervising and teaching skills in making new pilots.

The Spin Scenario

The spin endorsement is often a rushed-by, ill-prepared lesson. The spin should build confidence in aircraft control and teach maneuverability.

Table 7-2. Judgement Scenario Database examples

Scenario	A	B	C	D
Your soon-to-graduate instrument candidate has asked for a lesson in icing. He would like to experience ice on his C-172 so that he can learn the flight characteristics. What will you do?	Choose a cold VFR day with an overcast layer, low tops and sunny above. You plan to porpoise in and out of the tops.	Choose a cold day with low scattered to broken clouds. You plan to fly though the middle of the layer.	Choose a day with reported light icing and 800-1,000 ceiling. You plan to conduct local IFR approaches.	Instructing a pilot to fly in icing conditions sends the wrong message. Instruct the candidate that a C-172 should never be in the ice.
You witness a pilot taxiing to the ramp at a speed that is unsafe and too fast. This is not your pilot. You know his instructor, although he is not at the airport today. What do you do?	Enlighten the pilot, instructing him in proper taxi technique.	Say nothing to the pilot. Call the other instructor and report to him what you saw.	Mind you own business. This clearly does not involve you. He was probably just late in returning the plane.	Challenge the pilot and point out his reckless behavior. However, let his instructor, instruct him.
All things being equal and control surfaces in the neutral position, if you were able to have control of only one of the following, which would you choose?	Elevator	Ailerons	Rudder	Com Radio
It's been a hectic Saturday at the flight school with pilots scheduled back-to-back and tomorrow looks like more of the same. You find that you are slipping behind schedule, later and later for your next appointment. What will do you?	Forego the paperwork. You can get caught up on documentation during the next rainy day.	Ask the dispatcher to call your last appointment and postpone his time for one hour so you can catch up.	Ask the dispatcher to reassign a flight from your schedule to another instructor's so that you can get caught up.	Work an hour later after your appointments to get caught up, even if you aren't paid for this time.
Your soon-to-graduate, instrument candidate is expecting a flight lesson to review partial panel. The weather is 800 overcast and 3 miles visibility. You will be in the clouds during your lesson. What will you do?	Conduct the lesson as planned. It's great that you are able to offer a partial panel experience in actual conditions.	Conduct the lesson as planned. Inform ATC of your intent to practice partial panel and stay in radar contact for extra protection.	Conduct a different lesson that provides benefitial training in actual conditions.	Cancel the flight. Training in IMC is not safe. Conduct a ground review in prep for the practical exam.
Your private-pilot-candidate has asked you to demonstrate a spin. You have not done a spin since your initial CFI training, 3 years ago. What will you do?	Decline to demonstrate the spin and offer to introduce your student to another CFI who can do a safe demonstration.	Decline to demonstrate the spin, explain the hazards of performing spins and offer extra practice in stall recognition and recovery.	Locate a senior CFI whom you trust to get you proficient and confident again with spins, and then demonstrate the maneuver to your candidate.	Rent a plane and go practice a few spins to refresh yourself on the entry, maneuver and recovery, and then demonstrate the maneuver to your candidate.
You have been asked to conduct a BFR for a longtime customer in his Lancair, a single engine, fixed-gear, airplane you've never flown before, having next generation avionics you've never seen before. The customer is legal, current and able to act and log PIC. What will you do?	Decline the job. Even if the customer is able to be PIC, you are not willing to find yourself in a situation you may not feel confident in handling.	Accept the job, but remain in day and VMC conditions.	Accept the job, only after you receive a flight check from the qualified instructor experienced in the Lancair, located 200 miles away.	Accept the job only after you have had the opportunity to fly the plane for yourself and to familiarize yourself with its unique characteristics and equipment.

Flight Mission: Your pilot is recovering from a stall but in the excitement of the moment he is holding pressure on one rudder pedal. Do you know what to expect or will you be surprised? Next, he is so eager to apply power that he adds full throttle before reducing the angle of attack. Are you ready?

The instructor will demonstrate a full spin with fully-developed rotations and he will make the recovery. Next, the instructor will demonstrate spin entries from a slipping turn and from a skidding turn. The final spin entry is conducted by the misapplication of power during a stall recovery. Then, the instructor will develop spin entries of various types, allowing you to recover from each. If you'd enjoy more practice with fully-developed spins, just say so. The instructor is able to teach you accuracy spins, rolling out on a selected landmark!

That doesn't sound too scary. It even sounds interesting. This lesson allows the CFI candidate to experience the full spin, not just the entry-attitude. It prepares him for the spin-entry that ducks under as well as the surprise of the spin-entry over the top.

Most instructors are too eager to apply power during a stall recovery in attempts at minimum altitude loss. They don't understand how easy it is for pilots to enter a spin on dual or solo lessons with misapplication of power.

Effective Instruction

Effective instruction means that the CFI candidate uses the general rules of good human relations. He is able to demonstrate maneuvers flawlessly while providing an explanation, which is clear, concise, and appropriate for the pilot's level of training. Instruction must be technically correct and complete—without prompting. The candidate must apply the fundamentals of instruction in developing the pilot's potential. He must recognize and correct common pilot errors. Additionally, he must supervise pilot technique in maintaining safe flight, including proactive traffic avoidance.

The candidate must never use any action, or lack of action, that requires a corrective action or intervention by the instructor. Lack of student supervision is unsatisfactory performance. The candidate's inability to allow the pilot to make and learn from errors which do not adversely affect the safety of flight is unsatisfactory performance. During preflight and post-flight activities, the candidate must use appropriate supervision of the pilot's application of aeronautical knowledge and skills. A flight mission that teaches effective instruction might look like this:

Teaching Mission: You will be assigned a flight lesson to teach and a pilot to teach it to. You are to prepare an effective scenario to accomplish the goals of the assigned lesson and you must provide a preflight briefing of no more than 20 minutes. Your preflight briefing must inspire the pilot to higher thinking skills. It must apply aeronautical knowledge.

You will supervise the pilot in obtaining a local weather briefing and help him to make the correct go/no-go decision using real data. You will supervise the pilot **practicing** preflight inspection, engine start, run-up, radio communications, and taxi. You must recognize and correct his errors.

During flight, you must provide opportunities for the pilot to use decision-making skills that are appropriate for his level of training. After takeoff, you will first teach then supervise appropriate aspects of the scenario as you planned it. Incorporate available technology that is appropriate to the pilot's level of training. You are expected to supervise the pilot **practicing** terrain and traffic avoidance and obstacle clearance.

After the flight you will conduct a learner-centered evaluation. It must be fair and accurate, but positive in nature. Record an entry for the pilot's logbook and assign relevant homework.

It's a lot to ask of a candidate. But until he can demonstrate his preparedness to be effective as a teacher in producing safe pilots, he's not ready for the privileges of a flight instructor certificate.

Preparing for First Solo

A lesson that teaches the CFI candidate to determine if a pilot is ready for first solo must encompass much more than the touchdown. The candidate must be taught to consider the pilot's eligibility, and decision-making skills. A teaching mission could look like this:

Teaching Mission: The CFI candidate will be assigned a flight lesson and a pilot to teach. Your pilot is preparing to solo and is subject to stress, anxiety, and unexpected defense mechanisms. You must deal with them.

You are to prepare an effective scenario to accomplish the goals of the assigned lesson and you must provide a preflight briefing of no more than 20 minutes. Your preflight briefing must inspire the pilot to higher thinking skills and should apply aeronautical knowledge and appropriate regulations.

You will supervise the pilot in obtaining a local weather briefing and help him make the correct go/no-go decision using real data. You will supervise the pilot **managing** the preflight inspection, engine start, run-up, radio communications, and taxi. You must recognize and correct his errors.

During flight, you must provide opportunities for the pilot to use decision-making skills that are appropriate for this level of training. After takeoff, you will first teach then supervise appropriate aspects of the scenario as you planned it. Incorporate available technology as appropriate. You are expected to supervise the pilot **managing** ATC requests, terrain, traffic, and obstacle clearance.

You must use accurate observations to correctly determine if the pilot is eligible and ready to conduct his first solo flight.

After the flight you will lead a learner-centered evaluation. It must be fair and accurate, but positive in nature. Record a proper entry in the pilot's logbook and assign relevant homework.

In this lesson, the CFI candidate should not be flying. He should be directing and supervising. At this stage of the candidate's training, he should be getting more comfortable in allowing the pilot to make safe mistakes. He should be capable of preventing instructional surprises. He should be comfortable with supervision. In this way, the candidate learns how to supervise pilot skills.

From Instructor-in-Training to Professional

After the CFI candidate is taught how to teach flying, the last step is to prepare him to be a working professional in the industry. The transition from candidate to working instructor is a difficult transition, requiring the highest decision-making skills. Often, in accepting a new job he moves away from the support of family and friends. He finds himself living in a new location, and flying unfamiliar airplanes. Help prepare the CFI candidate for his first teaching job with scenarios like the following.

Getting Hired Scenario

The waiver came today from the insurance company! Finally, I'll be allowed to fly the Cirrus! The flight school is in need of instructors, with pilots waiting to begin training, so the flight school manager requested a waiver to get me insured with less than the required hours.

It's about time; I need to start making some money. I have student loans to pay off. I don't know where the insurance company gets the right to make requirements so high to fly this little airplane. It has four seats, just like the Piper I'm used to. It's a low-wing. I've had plenty of experience flying at school. I graduated with top honors from Prestigious University and that should sure count for something. How else am I supposed to get flight experience? There's nothing I can do about the system. I'm just glad the flight school manager didn't ask to look at my logbook entries.

Now I can show them I am as good—no, that I am better than the average Joe. I'm sure that I'll quickly move up to the twin. I can't wait to get my hands on some bigger equipment. I just have to suffer through this for about six months, and then I am set for the airlines.

The winds are pretty bad tonight but I've flown in higher winds than this. Most of the guys have been canceling lessons. I can't believe how all the planes are distorted in their tie down positions and tugging against the ropes. Oh well. I just wish my first Cirrus student tonight wasn't Sour Dr. Smith. What a jerk. He's as old as my father and as dumb as an ox. Oh well, lookout Doc, your flying ace is here![2]

Discussion Questions: Did you perceive any risks that the instructor did not consider? Which hazardous attitudes dominate his thinking? What are the antidotes? Do you think the flight school manager made the right decision in asking for a waiver for this instructor? Why do you think the insurance company sets pilot requirements where they are? Will he be an effective instructor for Dr. Smith? Is he servicing the flight school? The industry? Dr. Smith? Would you take instruction from him?

Getting Promoted Scenario

It was the end of a tough week and the young CFI had already put in a full day's flight instruction. He was hitching a ride home in a company plane. It was his college homecoming football weekend and he had fifty-yard-line tickets with college buddies.

When he got to the aircraft, he discovered that there wasn't a seat for him. The plane was configured with pilot seat only, for hauling cargo. He inquired about an extra seat and was told that none was available, but that the co-pilot seatbelt attached to the floor could be used.

He had not been with this company very long and had never run into this situation before. Unfortunately, the pilot he was to ride with had a reputation for flying an aerobatic freighter. He couldn't recall the regulation so wasn't sure if he needed a seat or not, but decided it must be okay or the company wouldn't let him do it. Besides, he wanted to get home. But more than that, he wanted the chance to buddy up to this pilot for possible future freight-flying experience.

He wasn't checked out in the specific make and model aircraft, but he could easily note the peculiarities in his pilot's procedures. Being a "lower pilot" wanting to move up, he did not dare say anything. He wanted the pilot to like him and to recommend him for a position in the charter department.[3]

Discussion Questions: Assess the risks and discuss why the instructor went on this flight in terms of: (1) Knowledge (2) Physical (3) Financial (4) Legal (5) Egocentric (6) Sociologic (7) Benefits vs. Risks. What was the only real decision that the instructor had to make? What are the hazardous attitudes showing in his decision-making? How do you feel about working at this company? What are the risks to the instructor should he get his wish and be promoted to charter pilot? Does he have another choice?

Conclusions

In the 1964 movie "My Fair Lady" Professor Higgins bets that he can train the Cockney flower girl Eliza to pass as a duchess. Because of Higgins' high regard for the girl's abilities and his commitment to her transformation, she acquires the traits of a duchess, and others treat her accordingly.

The message here is about how an instructor impacts the performance of his pupil. If the instructor's expectations are high, pupils stretch to meet those expectations. When expectations are low, for whatever reason, the message is received and they perform as anticipated. Instructors can use the power of positive expectations to raise the bar and drive higher performance.

The CFI candidate trained in the course outlined in this chapter had training goals defined within standards adopted by industry rather than against minimum standards.

A course of training steeped in scenarios that promote risk management and reduce instructional surprises gives the CFI candidate a head start on making decisions relative to pilot training. Most candidates mistakenly believe that after certification is when they'll learn to become good instructors, after having conducted several hours of dual instruction. This implies that paying customers of our industry would receive less than standard training while the new instructor gains experience. "Improper Student Supervision" is a term the NTSB uses on too many incident reports to explain an instructional flight gone wrong.

The instructor has options that require his decisions. Today it may be a go-around on landing, tomorrow it could be to instruct in an unfamiliar technically-advanced aircraft. Young, goal-oriented flight instructors sometimes lose sight of the available options. This is an important concept for all CFI candidates before entering the work environment.

Exercises

1. In consideration of student supervision, think of the first time you solo your first student. She has only 13 hours of flight. List specifically the limitations you would place in her logbook for future solo flights.

2. The author mentions the "legal, ethical and professional issues on the business side of flight instructing." Discuss in a five-page paper what you feel are the issues on the business-side of flight instructing.

3. Research NTSB accidents for five examples of "improper instructor supervision" during dual flight training in an aircraft make and model you routinely fly. Discuss any trends or insights in a short paper.

Chapter 8

Weather In Scenarios

Weather-related accidents continue to be problematic for general aviation pilots and no other subject is more fitting for scenario-based training.

Weather Knowledge Challenge

Surveys have shown that participants, including flight instructors, believe they have a good, general understanding of weather and a broad base of aviation weather knowledge. However, in one study participants did not demonstrate an understanding of weather "as it pertains to real flight operations." The study concluded that pilots do not have "accurate perceptions regarding their levels of weather knowledge… and cannot be expected to acquire it on their own as they gain more flight experience."[1]

The study showed:

    I.   Causes of Weather/Weather Patterns. The average correct score was 65%.

    II.   Weather Hazards. The average score was 83%.

    III.   Weather Services. The average score was 51%.

    IV.   Weather Regulations. The average score was 61%.

    V.   Weather Interpretation. The average score was 55%.

    VI.   Weather-Related Decision Making. The average score was 77%.

The survey data illuminates what is needed in weather-related education. Instructors can compile this information in an "as needed" teaching format according to the pilot's level of training. Finally, personal minimums will give pilots a wide safety-net in making weather related decisions.

Weather at Solo

At the solo phase of flight training, pilots must possess the knowledge of weather regulations and information pertaining to local flying and the go/no-go decision. At this point, "the information of most concern to pilots pertains to the wind, cloud ceiling and the visibility." [2] The pilot's mindset is, "Can I go fly?" With instructor supervision, the pilot is helped to make a good decision. A preflight briefing might look similar to the list in Figure 8-1.

Meteorology	Computerized weather briefing

❑ Definition of ceiling. Cloud layers.
❑ Visibility. Common obscurations to visibility.
❑ Wind direction. Velocity/Gusts
❑ METAR and TAF
❑ Weather minimums for your current level of training. Review flight school safety procedures and weather minima.
❑ Always get good weather briefings. But once airborne, believe what you see.
 	
A telephone weather briefing
❑ How to ask for a wx briefing
❑ Writing it down. Format/shorthand and abbreviations
❑ Go or no go—not based solely on FSS recommendations
❑ It's okay to ask FSS to repeat information
❑ Get what you need. Be persistent
	❑ DUATS
	   ❑ Getting a logon and password
	   ❑ Screen entries for a standard weather briefing
	   ❑ Reading coded weather
	   ❑ Standard format for METAR and TAF
	   ❑ Printing
	❑ aviationweather.gov/ADDS—better radar
	❑ Not all Internet weather sites are suitable for pilot briefings.
	
	Scenario
	❑ Pilot calls FSS and obtains a weather briefing for flight in local area. Instructor is at hand to supervise, but does not assist.
	
	In flight
	❑ Apply what was on paper to what is seen in flight.

Homework Call or logon at home and receive weather briefings. Compare the weather to what is seen outside.	

Figure 8-1. Preflight weather briefing

Weather at Solo Cross-Country

During the solo cross-country phase of training, weather decision-making opportunities are expanded. The pilot's mindset is revised and is characterized as "Can I reach my destination or not?"

Emphasis during training is on the continued evaluation of changes in weather conditions and a new plan to deal with those changes. "A pilot may make a series of good decisions, but… the flight is only as safe as the last decision. A safe pilot is a proactive pilot." [3] Instructors assess the pilot's decision-making skills by asking pilots to think aloud as they make weather-related decisions.

Mindset at Graduation and Beyond

Understanding weather as a whole and the "consideration of multiple factors, simultaneously" is the final result of a safe, weather-minded pilot. At this phase, the pilot's mindset regarding weather-related decisions should be characterized as "Should I continue the flight as planned or not?" [4]

Organize a PowerPoint presentation, constructing a scenario for a cross-country flight. Provide natural points throughout the flight to ask the pilot for a continue/divert/land decision. Points for decision making might include: 1) before leaving the flight planning room, 2) before takeoff, 3) hourly enroute updates, 4) before initial descent, and 5) before beginning approach.

This method encourages a constant state of vigilance by the pilot to detect changes—a kind of "problem vigil." It promotes situational awareness and helps the pilot learn to organize information so that he may recognize changes and diagnose what, if any, revision should be made to any aspect of the flight.

At Cirrus Owners and Pilot's Association (COPA) training programs, participants are encouraged to "STOP and THINK." During the problem vigil, participants *Stop* and *Think* about the:

- Flight **P**lan
- **P**lane
- **P**ilot
- **P**assengers
- **P**rogramming of cockpit technology

Integrating the Weather Scenario

A weather scenario should require pilots to integrate information over different areas, interpreting the information, and demonstrating an understanding of how the information affects a real flight.

A great scenario-based weather training program can feature weather topics using presentation software like PowerPoint. As the scenario unveils itself, events begin to build the accident chain in small, barely noticeable ways—just as it does in real life. For example: the departure time was delayed while waiting for fuel, ground speed was slowed by 5 knots from planned, weather begins a slight deterioration, and there is a short ATC delay of some sort. Add to that the small inconvenience of a nonessential cockpit technology failure, and a passenger that is impatient.

Pilots are encouraged to consider questions such as, what has changed since we last made our decisions about the 5 P's? What are the major risk factors now? How does the change affect us now and how will it affect the duration of the flight? Are we comfortable with the effect? Is an accumulation of issues starting…an accident chain? What resources in the cockpit do we have that can be used to assist us? What additional information would we like to have? From where or whom can we obtain this information? How can we solicit help? What resource do we wish we had? What can we do to improve our situation? Should we abort the flight, continue as planned, or continue with a diversion?

In the perfect scenario, the pilot is asked to consider the weather pattern and its hazards; to use weather services; to apply weather regulations; to interpret weather data; and to make the ultimate continue, divert or abort weather-related decision. Two keys for successful weather scenarios are essential:

1. Changes should be subtle and realistic. Changes shouldn't be overly complicated and shouldn't overload the pilot. The mission of the weather scenario is in decision making more so than emergency training.

2. The scenario should not present the problem, rather it should present the symptom as the pilot would experience it in flight. The instructor should not offer "you have ice on your wings" instead, the symptom is that the airspeed in dropping and/or the autopilot is becoming sluggish, etc.

Two great examples are available online at the FAA FITS presentations website:

http://www.faa.gov/education_research/training/fits/presentations/media/scenario.ppt

http://www.faa.gov/education_research/training/fits/presentations/media/SRM%20scenario.ppt

Download these presentations, and study them. Once the "recipe" is understood, making revisions appropriate to terrain, aircraft, weather patterns and pilots is easy. An IFR icing condition in a deice-equipped cabin-class twin is a different scenario than the same icing condition in an older C-172 without GPS or datalink. Even small weather issues are cumbersome if the pilot is circumnavigating busy Bravo airspace or high terrain. Revise the takeoff time in the scenario to just before sunset or sunrise, giving new opportunities for the pilot to deal with fog. Change the takeoff time to a hot August afternoon, giving the pilot opportunities to deal with high winds and thunderstorms.

A presentation like PowerPoint is ideal for weather scenarios. It allows the instructor to introduce complicated situations, giving practice in complex decisions and decision-trees. Most flight-training environments are highly structured and controlled, but weather in the real world is not. The PowerPoint scenario may be the best way—outside of the actual conditions—to train and evaluate pilot decision-making because it allows training in complex situations.

The presentation might include a DUATS-type weather briefing, a completed NavLog and charts. Be creative, but keep it real. Keep it simple. Supplement the scenario experience with handouts or other take-home materials. What's important is the "experience" of the scenario and its realism.

Top 10 Safe Weather Strategies

Fly in the weather at all levels of training. Fly in the rain. Fly in the snow. Instead of using a hood in training private pilot candidates during flight-by-reference-to-instruments, fly in real clouds. Give instrument candidates plenty of actual time in the clouds. With ATC's help, request block altitudes for practice. Instructors should have flown in all conditions before taking a paying customer into the weather.

The number-one cause of weather-related accidents is continued VFR into instrument conditions. Most of these accidents occur to pilots who are instrument-rated. Only by flying in the real weather and experiencing changing weather conditions will pilots learn to interpret enroute weather cues, use up-to-date weather sources and properly diagnose adverse weather.

Common VFR into IMC accident scenarios include improper judgment of deteriorating weather, scud running, underestimating the risks involved with flight into deteriorating conditions, overconfidence in coping with conditions, social pressures that influence weather-related decisions, and inadequate preflight of the weather. During training, seek out strategies to incorporate these Top 10 Safe Weather Strategies:[5]

1. Obtain weather from all available sources prior to the flight and update weather information enroute using Datalink, Nexrad or other, traditional forms of weather sources.
2. Vary the planned route because of the new weather information.
3. Land and refuel to increase flight endurance for turning back or diverting options.
4. Vary the planned route because of the weather en route.
5. Land and wait for the weather to improve.

6. Plan ahead, evaluate the next stage of flight to assess expected weather ahead.

7. Turn back.

8. Perform two 360-degree turns to think and assess.

9. Re-configure the aircraft for a slow speed to think and assess.

10. Carry out a precautionary landing.

Pilot Weather Personal Minimums

Much has been said about personal minimums. Helping the pilot understand his motivations for flying and how his motivations affect his decisions about the go/no-go decision pertaining to weather is key. Use a checklist like the following:

____What is your current personal minimum for VFR visibility?

____What is your current personal minimum for VFR ceiling?

____Are these minimums rock-solid or do you adjust them depending on circumstances?

____Does the distance you have to fly through bad weather affect your willingness to take off? (You can define bad weather for yourself.)

____If you were given incentive to take off, would this affect your willingness to takeoff in conditions less than your minimums?

____Would having passengers affect your willingness to take off?

____If you had an additional 100 hours of flight time, would that affect your willingness to take off?

____No matter what the weather is supposed to be, believe what you see and react early.

Conclusions

"The nature of the general aviation environment is such that pilots are expected to operate in an uncertain and risky operational domain where they are confronted with a range of meteorological phenomena about which a series of in-flight decisions need to be made." [6]

Pilots trained in a scenario-based situation are better equipped to make smarter in-flight decisions and to have a level confidence appropriate for their current skill and experience. Good weather-related scenarios that require a sound weather education, realistic assessment of one's skills, and the exercise of personal minimums are the keys to teaching better weather-related decisions.

There are no specifically "weather-only" scenarios in this chapter because weather is but one ingredient in all scenarios. Instructors should not attempt to construct "weather-only" scenarios, where the weather is the sole subject matter to deal with. Rather, all scenarios should include the elements of weather, as appropriate to the pilot's current mindset.

Exercises

1. Collect online METARs, TAFs and other weather products that may be useful for an upcoming scenario. Choose a challenging but flyable day.

2. Download the sample scenarios mentioned in the chapter and study them.

3. Write a realistic, VFR scenario of 1-hour in duration, appropriate to your training environment, including appropriate elements of weather.

4. Identify which phase of training the scenario is appropriate for. (When will you use it?)

5. Identify the pilot decision-making opportunities within the scenario.

6. Write a detailed script enabling the instructor to properly facilitate the scenario. Be sure to identify the underlying concepts that may not be immediately obvious.

7. Choose current, commercially available handouts to supplement the scenario.

Chapter 9

The Right Attitude

Hazardous Attitude	Antidote
Anti-Authority	*Follow the rules, they are usually right.*
Impulsivity	*Not so fast, think first.*
Invulnerability	*It could happen to me.*
Macho	*Taking chances is foolish.*
Resignation	*I'm not helpless. I can make a difference.*

The Hazardous Attitudes and their Antidotes

The FAA identifies five attitudes hazardous to flying, as well as their "antidotes." Most pilots have at least one. Hazardous attitudes can lead to poor decision making and actions involving unnecessary risks. Pilots are asked to examine their decisions, ensuring that they have not been influenced by one of these attitudes. They are then expected to become familiar with alternatives, or antidotes that specifically counteract the hazardous attitudes. During flight, pilots must be able to "recognize a hazardous attitude, correctly label the thought, and recall its antidote"[1] before their impact on decisions leads to a bad day. It sounds easy.

The topic of hazardous attitudes is an important one that many instructors are too often uncomfortable teaching. There may be two fundamental reasons:

1. Most young, new flight instructors feel intimidated when saying to an older professional person, "You have a hazardous attitude," and don't know the right words to use.
2. Many instructors view it as the "touchy-feely" side of aviation. They don't feel qualified to talk about the headwork.

Unfortunately there are few practical teaching tools to bring the concept of hazardous attitudes into practical application. Training manuals are riddled with mnemonics: DECIDE, I'M SAFE, CARE, PAVE, 3Ps, 5Ps, TEAM. After a while it becomes a blur. Too often such slogans merely pay lip service, just to get through the FAA Knowledge Exam.

Instead of promoting slogans, develop real skills that lead to safety being a part of the culture. Teach self-assessment so that the student will know which hazardous attitudes are at play. It's a more professional approach to a vital topic in flight training: begin with a personal self-assessment, then practice recognition and recovery. End with practical scenarios to put it to work in the cockpit. Include this training for pilots at all levels to emphasize the importance of ongoing re-assessment.

A Personal Assessment

In the accident prevention pamphlet *Introduction to Pilot Judgment,* the FAA promotes a Personal Assessment of Hazardous Attitudes. It is an inventory of 10 situations. The pilot reads each and selects a decision regarding the situation. This allows a glimpse into how the concept of hazardous attitudes applies in the cockpit. While the situations represent extreme cases, they are presented in simplified form in order to help the pilot easily identify each attitude.

As a result, the pilot learns which of his own thoughts most often match a hazardous attitude. Through these illustrated patterns, the pilot can see the trends that occur in his own decision-making. It shows which hazardous attitudes the pilot's personality tends toward, and therefore which behaviors he should be watching out for to avoid them.

This assessment is also available online at www.avhf.com, "Evaluation." The self-assessment is a more comfortable way to start a discussion about hazardous attitudes with a pilot who seems reluctant or overly sensitive about a personal assessment being made for him by others.

Recognition and Recovery

Becoming proficient in recognizing a hazardous attitude and replacing it with a good one requires repetition and practice. However, many pilots are unable or unwilling to recognize hazardous attitudes in themselves. The following scenarios illustrate hazardous attitudes in other pilots. Reviewing scenarios in dual ground briefings or as assigned homework allows the pilot to practice and develop skills in recognition and recovery. There is no one right answer. Different pilots see the situations differently. What is most important is the debriefing discussion that allows the pilot to consider hazardous attitudes in normal flight situations.

VFR: You are flying with a pilot friend on a one-hour flight to an unfamiliar, rural airport. The last FSS update included a "VFR not recommended" for the possibility of fog at the destination. Your pilot momentarily considered returning home where the visibility was good, but quickly decided to continue. Why do you think he decided to continue?

1. He hated to admit that he couldn't complete the intended flight.
2. He resented the suggestion by flight service that he should change his mind.
3. He felt sure that things would turn out safely, and that there was no real danger.
4. He reasoned that since his actions wouldn't make a difference, he may as well continue.
5. He felt the need to decide quickly so he took the simplest alternative.

IFR: You were invited to ride along on a friend's flight. He is the pilot-in-command. Nearing the end of the long flight, your destination airport is reporting a ceiling of 800 feet and 1 mile visibility, fog and haze. You have just heard a Cessna 182 miss the approach (ILS minimums are 200 and ½). Your pilot friend decided to attempt the ILS approach. Why do you think he decided to continue?

1. Ceiling and visibility estimates are often not accurate.
2. He is a better pilot, with better equipment than the one who just missed the approach.
3. While here, might as well try. He might get lucky.
4. He was tired and just wanted to land now.

5. He's been successful in completing approaches under these circumstances in the past.

The above scenarios do not infer that pilots shouldn't fly when VFR is not recommended or attempt an instrument approach with 800/1 conditions. The scenarios only represent flights in conditions that warrant extra care and thought in the decision process. They ensure that the decisions are made from real data and are not being influenced by hazardous attitudes.

The next scenario (Figure 9-1) illustrates hazardous attitudes in flight. The numbered sentences provide easy reference in the discussion that follows.

(1) I had been at 13,500 for about 20 minutes before descent. (2) I did not have supplemental oxygen. (3) I didn't think anything would happen because I'd done it several times before and things always turned out okay. (4) My altitude was below 12,000 for about 40 minutes before I began my landing approach. (5) When I got over the runway threshold, I was a little "foggy" about how to land the plane. (6) I guess "confused" would be a better word. (7) Well, because of my slow and foggy thinking, the plane got ahead of me. (8) I tried to land anyway, wanting to get on the ground as soon as possible. (9) The next thing I knew I was porpoising down the runway. (10) The first jolt scared the stuffing out of me. (11) But surprisingly, it also made me more alert. (12) I got the airplane airborne again in the go-around. (13) My second landing attempt was better but rough as my head was still fuzzy. (14) I was lucky. (15) I went to see my doctor right away. (16) He asked me what I had eaten before the flight. (17) I recalled my last meal was 12 hours before and was only a candy bar. (18) He said, "Your story sounds like hypoxia (lack of oxygen) or hypoglycemia (low blood sugar) or both." (19) "I suspect both because you continued to feel confused at the lower altitudes." (20) "Also your symptoms cleared rapidly after your first landing attempt." (21) "A surge of adrenalin in such a situation will produce very rapid increase in blood sugar level." (22) "However, the hypoxia may have made the blood sugar problem more severe." (23) I left his office a wiser pilot. (24) I assured him that before flying I would eat a proper meal. (25) I also promised to get supplemental oxygen for future high-altitude flights.

Figure 9-1. Hazardous thinking

Discussion Questions *(Circle your answer):*

The hazardous attitude best describing the pilot's thinking in sentence 3 is:

Anti-authority   Impulsivity   Invulnerability   Resignation

The subject area mentioned in sentence 5 is:

Pilot   Aircraft Environment   Pilot/Environment

Which sentence suggests the hazardous attitude impulsivity?

7   8   9   10

Which antidote would you suggest for what the pilot is saying in sentence 14?

"It could happen to me."   "Not so fast, think first."

"Taking chances is foolish."   "I'm not helpless, I can make a
                                   difference."

What combination of subject areas does sentence 18 suggest?

Pilot/Aircraft   Pilot/Environment

Aircraft/Environment   Pilot/Aircraft/Environment

What does sentence 19 suggest about the doctor?

He knows his patient.
He doesn't know anything about airplanes
He knows about psychiatry and psychology.
He understands flight physiology and its affects on pilot judgment.

For which subject area has the pilot gained a greater respect as indicated by sentence 24?

Pilot   Aircraft   Environment   Pilot/Aircraft

Effective risk management requires a pilot to constantly re-evaluate risk in flight. Otherwise the likelihood of a safe, fun flight is reduced. Which sentence is an example of the pilot's lack of risk assessment/ management?

1   2   3   5

One Lesson Plan to Teach Hazardous Attitudes

Chapter 2 referred to an ADM "ground briefing." Hazardous attitudes as part of the total aeronautical decision making concept should be taught early in the pilot's training. But don't stop there. Keep coming back to the subject as it applies in later discussions. Additional hazardous attitude recognition practice can be inserted into a review of accident and incident reports.

Here is a complete list of discussion points that can be used during a one-hour briefing to effectively cover hazardous attitudes and apply them to the cockpit:

1. Prior to the ground briefing on Hazardous Attitudes, assign as homework the online "Personal Assessment" and the FAA handout, Introduction to Pilot Judgment. Then during the briefing,
2. Review the pilot's self-assessment.
3. Review the FAA pamphlet, including the topics:
   a. Pilot Responsibility
   b. Defining Judgment
   c. Judgment Concepts: The Poor-Judgment Chain
   d. The Three Mental Processes of a Safe Flight
   e. Identifying and Reducing Stress
4. Don't rely solely on FARs as the safety benchmark. Just because it's legal doesn't make it safe.
5. Introduce the Risk-Management Checklist.
6. Personal minimums and social influences in decision making
7. Review two hazardous attitudes.
8. Assign as homework the six hazardous attitudes scenarios for the pilot to review.

Attitudes in Advanced Training

Hazardous attitudes are also part of advanced training. Assign the pilot to complete the Self-Assessment, even if he's done it in the past. With time and experience, attitudes change. Make a case for continuous self assessment. It marks growth in a new pilot and points out complacency in seasoned pilots. Complete the ADM briefing. Even if the pilot has had the briefing before, make a case for reviewing the basics and the discipline for managing hazardous attitudes. Just change the scenarios to what is appropriate for the level of pilot.

#1 Flight Review Hazardous Attitude Scenario: The pilot is a 30-year-old Arizona firefighter, nearing completion of his instrument rating. He has 3.8 hours night experience. On Tuesday, he puts in a full shift at work then drives two hours to an airport to rent a plane. He intends to fly back home, pick up his family and continue to Memphis, TN for Thanksgiving.

A friend is waiting at an enroute rest stop, where the pilot makes three attempts at a downwind landing before barely getting the airplane stopped on the 3,500-foot runway. The pilot unloads his wife and daughters, ages 5 and 3 years old. The friend suggests spending the night. The pilot says he's in a hurry to beat a cold front to Memphis. He has plenty of fuel so he departs without adding fuel, filing a flight plan, or getting update weather.

Approaching Memphis, ATC informs him about a ceiling developing at 3,000 feet with fog rolling in underneath. They are on top.

What hazardous attitude(s) is the firefighter practicing? Do you think he's used to accepting risks in his daily life? Do you think he will attempt to land at Memphis? List all the ways he has put his passengers at risk from the beginning of his flight.

#2 Flight Review Hazardous Attitude Scenario: A physician in his late fifties owns two aircraft. He practices at several rural hospital clinics within 100 miles of home. He is in the habit of flying to work three times a week. The doctor has suffered three heart attacks, one of which hospitalized him for two months and the most recent one was less than six months ago. He recently moved his planes from the small airport near his home to a larger airport where he leases the aircraft to the flight school. He continues to fly although it is not known if he has a current medical.

Which hazard attitude(s) is the physician practicing? Do you think he is used to accepting risks in his daily life? List all the ways his flying risks have changed recently.[2]

Conclusions

Every pilot has hazardous attitudes. It's not a choice but rather a part of one's personality. "There are controls for these attitudes, but to use them successfully requires continuous self-assessment." Managing hazardous attitudes requires practice at first, and then later, discipline. "The most important aspects of self-discipline are those of managing hazardous attitudes, workload, and stress. A professional requires good self-discipline and the wisdom to rise above human weaknesses." [3]

Exercises

1. Take the Personal Assessment of Hazardous Attitudes available online. Discuss in a short paper which hazardous attitude you tend toward and if you've seen evidence of this in your previous flight experience. What is the antidote?

2. Answer the discussion questions in #1 and #2 Flight Review Hazardous Attitude Scenarios.

3. Write a lesson plan that you feel comfortable using to discuss hazardous attitudes in a practical application format. Don't just define the attitudes and antidotes, but how you will work the topic into routine flight training lessons.

Chapter 10

Wisdom Report Scenarios

"Mix ignorance with arrogance at low altitude and the results are almost guaranteed to be spectacular."
—Bruce Landsberg
Executive Director of the AOPA Air Safety Foundation

Learning from the Mistakes

An ancient proverb proclaims, "A wise man learns from the mistakes of others. No one lives long enough to make them all himself." Such is the reasoning for including NTSB and ASRS reports in flight training. The National Transportation Safety Board (NTSB) collects and reports details of aviation accidents and incidents. The Aviation Safety Reporting System (ASRS) as defined by NASA collects, analyzes, and responds to voluntarily submitted aviation safety incident reports with the intent to help lessen the likelihood of aviation accidents.

The ASRS is administered by NASA; thus it has become known as "the NASA card" by many pilots. Internet access allows anyone interested in the causes of accidents and incidents to peruse these databases containing decades of flying mistakes made by others.

Any such report could be held as example of what not to do, and instructors often exploit these facts to illustrate how to learn from the mistakes of others. But if such training spotlights only the probable cause of the incident, then the conversation has presented learning only at the lowest, rote level. Such reports also offer opportunities to teach thinking skills.

Assuming pilots don't take off with the notion of having an accident, the question arises "Why did the pilot's decision seem like the right one at the time?" By considering the thought process of the accident-pilot, you can determine what information about the situation made the accident-pilot choose his action. Three techniques used by smart instructors move incident reports beyond the mere actions of the accident-pilot: *Share the Story*, *Build the Story*, and *Dissect the Story* puts accident-incident reports to use in different ways.

Share the Story

The first technique requires the instructor to share the accident facts. Consider this example:

> The pilot was positioning the airplane to pick up passengers at a remote airstrip. He reported low-level turbulence and strong winds during the approach and was unsure if he could complete the landing. As he turned the airplane onto final, the turbulence diminished, and he elected to land. There was a large pool of water on the runway, and he decided to land longer than normal in order to miss the water. Soon after passing the water pool, the airplane settled to the runway with the landing gear retracted. There were no mechanical problems with the airplane. The pilot said the gear up warning horn did not activate because of the increased power setting he used to fly over the pool of water. The NTSB determines the probable cause(s) as: The pilot's failure to follow the prelanding checklist which resulted in a wheels-up landing. A factor in the accident was the pilot's diverted attention associated with turbulence and a water pool.[1]

Telling the story imparts good lessons, but the fact that it is a true story makes it even more interesting. The instructor might say to the pilot, "See? This is why I want you to use the checklist and to always be primed for a go-around." But in doing so, the instructor loses the opportunity to encourage the pilot's higher-level thinking and decision making.

When you *Share the Story*, you promote the pilot's thinking by drawing him deeper into the incident. Have the pilot reflect on what the accident-pilot was thinking and why the actions seemed (at the time) like a good idea. Then, encourage our pilot picture himself in the same situation: under what circumstances could he see himself doing the same thing? Only when our pilot opens his mind to the possibility that it could happen to him can he begin to consider how his own thought progression could lead to a similar situation and actions. Subsequently, our pilot can correlate how his thinking ultimately affects his actions or reactions during a given situation. Consider the following discussion questions that the instructor could use to encourage our pilot's thinking:

- Remote airstrip: What type runway do you envision? What can you do to verify your impressions? What additional information would you like to have about the runway? How can you obtain additional information? Are your impressions different during the winter months? During summer?

- How do strong winds and/or turbulence affect your choices in landing at a short and/or narrow runway? Does changing your arrival time change the situation and options?

- Under what conditions would you choose to land at a remote strip? Under what conditions would you not?

- Why was the pilot concerned with landing in the standing water? Should it concern you? What could you do to improve your situation?

- What risk factors was the pilot attempting to avoid by landing beyond the water pool? Did the pilot have other choices for dealing with the water pool? What were they?

- The warning horn for the gear didn't sound because the pilot was flying with an unusually high power setting. What "warnings" are on the plane that may be affected by your decisions to operate outside your normal procedures?

- What are other ways that pilots become distracted on final approach? When flying a fixed-gear airplane, what types of things can go wrong because of last minute distractions? What would you do?

- This is a lesson in distractions. What can you do to avoid having a bad day after you've been distracted on short final?

Notice how the questions put our pilot into the situation? Our pilot is asked to consider risk factors as well as possible alternatives and the implications of choosing each. It makes you stop and think, doesn't it?

Share the Story is most effective in group settings when the ideas and insights of many participants combine for in-depth and interesting discussions. When sharing the story, present the incident docket and refer to the accident-pilot with respect. Download the applicable charts or airport data in order to give the pilot a chance to evaluate conditions that factored into the event. Curtail the temptation to think or say, "How stupid was that?"— especially when "that" was probably not the lesson. The goal in sharing the story is to give our pilots the opportunity to mentally prepare for situations that they may encounter in the future.

Used correctly, accident reports represent scenarios that offer real learning moments. However, hindsight promotes bias. When you are told that the facts originate from a NTSB or ARSA file, it's already obvious to you that something should have been done differently. So hindsight bias can be problematic when sharing the story.

Build the Story

When you *Build the Story* you don't precipitate hindsight bias. The benefit in this case is that our pilot is asked to think about the situation without being primed ahead of time on what not to do.

In building the story, the instructor introduces the accident conditions in the here-and-now for the pilot's consideration. The instructor does not share that the facts originated from NTSB or ASRS sources. Starting with the details from the same report used above in *Share the Story*, the instructor builds the story as a scenario:

> The instructor begins discussing with the pilot: Let's pretend you were the pilot positioning the airplane to pick up passengers at a remote airstrip. What are your thoughts about "remote airstrip?" What can you do to verify your impressions? What additional information would you like to have about the runway? How can you obtain additional information? Are your impressions different during the winter months? During summer?

> Now let's pretend that you encounter low-level turbulence and strong winds during the approach to the point that you're unsure you could complete the landing. What will you do? Remember, you have passengers waiting for you. What other options do you have? Is there anything that you could do to improve your situation? Under what conditions would you choose to land at a remote strip? When would you not?

> Well, let's pretend that after all that rocking and rolling, things seemed to calm down so that on final you decide to land, but you notice a large pool of standing water on the runway. What would you do? What risk factors are associated with that? What other options do you have?

> What "warnings" are on the plane that may be affected by your decisions to operate outside your normal procedures?

Build the Story is best used in one-on-one training situations and allows the instructor the added benefit of revising the story to fit the pilot's unique flying environment. However, it takes time for the story to unfold and for the pilot to consider his alternatives. Building the story may require more time than the instructor can invest in such a scenario.

Dissect the Story

The third technique in using accident reports requires the instructor to write a scenario one sentence at a time, and asks the pilot to dissect it likewise. It's most useful when including NTSB reports for self-study or homework. Consider the following weight and balance scenario.

Read the scenario and answer the questions that follow in Figure 10-1. The sentences in the scenario are numbered to help reference the questions that follow.

> (1) At takeoff the aircraft was about 20 pounds under maximum gross weight. (2) What I didn't realize was that the CG was slightly behind the aft limit. (3) The temperature was 93°F and the density altitude was 6,200 feet. (4) Because weight and balance had never created a problem for me in the past, I didn't bother to calculate my loading or my takeoff distance. (5) I did roughly estimate it in my head. (6) I thought it would probably take about a 1,600-foot takeoff roll. (7) My runway was 4,200 feet and I was sure there would be no problem. (8) The wind was from 260 at 8 knots so I took off from Runway 24. (9) During the takeoff roll, the airplane accelerated very slowly. (10) About halfway down the runway I considered aborting the takeoff. (11) I finally lifted off about two-thirds down the runway, and I figured it would probably be okay. (12) Then the real problem began. (13) As I established VY, the nose wanted to pitch way up. (14) Next, I noticed that I wasn't gaining enough altitude relative to the ridge, about a mile ahead. (15) Worried, I pulled the nose up further to Vx to try to climb faster. (16) The airplane was difficult to control. (17) As the ridge grew closer, my altitude over the ground was uncomfortably close. (18) The ridge was coming up and I knew I couldn't climb fast enough to clear it. (19) At one point my altitude over the ground was about 300 feet and I decided I had to turn around and go back. (20) The turn was very unnerving. (21) During the turn I think my wheels were about 20 feet over the tree tops. (22) But it was my only way out. (23) I was flying just above the stall speed and the airplane was very difficult to control. (24) I'm not sure how, but I was successful in making the airport.

Figure 10-1. Hazards and antidotes

- Which sentence indicates that the pilot didn't do something he should have?
- Which sentence indicates that the pilot did something too late?
- In sentence #1, which hazardous attitude does the pilot display?
- In sentence #11, which hazardous does the pilot display?
- In sentence #15, which hazardous attitude does the pilot display?
- The correct antidote for the hazardous attitude referred to in question #5 could be expected to call the pilot's attention to:

  —The rule about loading the heaviest passenger in the front.

  —The real possibility that overloading could cause a crash.

  —The possibility that a sudden change in attitude could cause a stall.

- The pilot, and not "lady luck," needs to do something quick.

- One principle of safety says that as time progresses, the alternatives available decrease and the opportunity to select the best alternative may be lost. Which sentence best illustrates this principle?

- Do you think the pilot fully evaluated the airplane during this event? Why?

- Do you think the pilot fully evaluated his environment during this event? Why?

Being General versus Getting Specific

When the lesson is one of general technique or knowledge, the geographic location of the incident, the type of plane involved or the flight experience of the pilot is not important. In such a lesson, the instructor can remove these facts from the scenario. Doing so ensures that our pilot doesn't get distracted by facts that aren't relative to the lesson.

On the other hand, if the lesson pertains to an aircraft checkout for a specific make and model, then the introduction of specific accident reports that relate to that airplane are appropriate. Often, reports concerning specific make and model aircraft can highlight trends in that airplane. For example, a C-210, although having a fuel endurance of six hours, has a high rate of fuel exhaustion incidents. Why would that be? The PA-34 Piper Seneca sees an inordinate number of pilots losing control and exiting the runway on takeoffs and landings.

> **Narrative:** I am colorblind and this is noted on my pilot certificate. The flight was from Duluth to Dallas with refueling in Kansas. Taking off from DLH, it was 2,500 OVC with a temp of 0 degrees. I started flying VFR at 2,000 feet under the overcast to stay out of icing conditions. Several holes appeared in the cloud deck allowing a climb to 6,500 feet as we neared Kansas. I was not sure if I could find a hole in the cloud deck, so I started to pick up an IFR clearance. The clouds became broken and I descended through a hole. At this point I unknowingly crossed a restricted area. I relied on the GPS to show special use airspace. The restricted area boundary lines were not visible against the background of the GPS. As I approached the airport, I called Kansas City Approach instead of the tower frequency. Hearing no response, I thought it was a CTAF and proceeded to the airport.

> **Synopsis:** A low-time pilot makes a series of errors including, probably, flight into IMC while VFR, entering a restricted area without permission and attempting to land without clearance, and relying on equipment he is not physically able to use.[2]

1. Which sentence indicates that the pilot didn't do something he should have?
2. Which sentence indicates that the pilot did something too late?
3. Which hazardous attitude(s) does the pilot display?
4. One principle of safety says that as time progresses, the alternatives available decrease and the opportunity to select the best alternative may be lost. Which sentence best illustrates this principle?
5. Do you think the pilot fully evaluated the airplane during this event? Why?
6. Do you think the pilot fully evaluated his environment during this event? Why?

In reviewing specific make and model reports, our pilot develops an awareness of operational considerations. By bearing in mind the particular aspects of a specific make and model in advance, the pilot's decisions will be faster and more effective in the event a high-stress situation should develop.

If a lesson concerns high-density altitude or mountainous terrain, then the instructor would choose reports that support that geography. If the lesson concerns, say, student-solo accidents, then introduce those reports. In any case, encourage the pilot to think beyond the facts of the report and get inside the accident-pilot's head. The real lesson is "How might you get trapped into the same thought processes, thus making the same decisions, leading to the same actions—and suffer the same outcome?"

Conclusions

Making good decisions and intuitively understanding the possible implications of our choices is difficult to do while simultaneously handling a chaotic situation. Reviewing NTSB reports with pilots during normal training activities helps prepare pilots by providing mental practice and rehearsal.

Share the story, build the story, or dissect the story, depending on the instructional activity. Use general or specific reports depending on the lesson. But less is more—an occasional accident review is enough to get important points across.

Exercises

1. Log onto the NTSB database and read what they had to say about our example, ANC03LA125.

2. Research and choose a general NTSB report that does not involve a fatality. Edit the incident report to remove those items that you don't feel are pertinent. Why aren't they?

3. Script your briefing with thought-provoking questions that promote higher-level thinking.

General NTSB Scenarios

DEN01FA030: The airplane was on a full ILS approach to Runway 18 at an airport with elevation 6,445 feet, in a mountainous area, at night. The control tower was closed. During non-tower operation hours, the airport used PCL on the tower frequency. The copilot made multiple attempts to turn on lights using the UNICOM frequency, which had been the CTAF until 6 months before. The captain continued his approach below IAP minimums without the runway lights being on. While in the landing flare, the captain reported that strong crosswinds and blowing snow created a "white-out" weather condition. The airplane touched down 195 feet left of the runway centerline in snow-covered terrain between the runway and taxiway. Two ILS 18 approach plates were found in the plane. One, out of date, showed UNICOM as the CTAF. The other was current and showed the tower frequency as CTAF.

Do you think that attempting to get the lights turned on was a distraction for the captain?

Did that distraction open the possibility for his possibly descending below minimums?

On approach, do you think the pilot was in radio communications with anyone?

Could ATC have helped answer the question of why the lights were not on?

What other equipment in the airplane is available to locate the proper frequencies?

Would you land after an IAP if you couldn't get the lights turned on? At what point would you abort?

This is also a lesson in resources management. When you need help, get it early.

ANC00LA029: The airplane collided with frozen pack ice, 3 miles from the airport, during a GPS IAP. Three-quarter-mile visibility, snow and fog were reported at the time of the accident. The pilot stated that he began a steep descent with the autopilot engaged. He indicated that as the airplane crossed the final approach course, the autopilot turned the airplane inbound toward the airport. He continued the steep descent, noted the airplane had overshot the course, and the autopilot was not correcting very well. He disengaged the autopilot and manually increased the correction heading to intercept the final approach course. During the descent he completed the landing checklist, extended the landing gear and flaps, and was tuning both the communications and navigation radios. The pilot said he looked up from tuning the radios to see the sea ice coming up too quickly to react, and impacted terrain. There were no pre-accident anomalies with the airplane.

Was this a stabilized approach?

Why would a pilot perform a "steep" descent into an airport?

At ¾ mile visibility, is there any room for distractions or abnormal procedures?

When would you have elected to abort the landing?

What are your personal minimums for a "steep descent?"

This is also a lesson in the accident chain. How many things went wrong for this pilot?

NYC01FA058: Pilot and passenger departed on a night IFR flight. Weather en route was a mix of IMC and VMC. When the airplane was 17 SW of its destination, the pilot was cleared for an IAP. At 9 miles, the pilot reported the airport in sight, and canceled IFR. The airplane continued to descend toward the airport on a modified left base until radar contact was lost at 3,300 feet MSL. The pilot was in radio contact with his wife just prior to the accident. He advised her that he was on base for Runway 32. Neither the pilot's wife, nor ATC, received a distress call from the pilot. The airplane was located the next morning. The accident site was 7.9 miles from the airport and 1,200 feet above airport elevation. Light snow showers were in the vicinity and satellite imagery showed that the airplane was operating under a solid overcast.

Does carrying passengers affect pilot decisions for continuing an approach?

Which do you think is riskier—VMC, IMC or a mix?

What are the implications of canceling IFR before short final? Why would you do that? Why not?

What are the implications of this pilot talking to his wife on the radio? Was this a distraction for the pilot?

What is the difference between remaining IFR and remaining on the IAP?

This is a lesson in following procedures. What is your personal policy regarding leaving an IAP procedure?

What is your personal policy about knowing the MSA during approach?

MIA99FA168: During taxi and takeoff on runway 9R, pilot and passengers stated the windows of the aircraft were fogged due to rain. The passengers could not see out the front windows. The pilot stated he could see out the front windows. The passengers also stated the pilot was holding the control wheel full to the right during takeoff. The winds were reported to be from 030 at 10 knots. During takeoff roll the aircraft drifted to the left and went off the runway. The aircraft then crossed over a taxiway and collided with a taxiway identifier sign. No windshear alerts were recorded and no standing water was observed on the runway.

How do you correct fog on the windows? How else?

Why couldn't the passengers see out the front windows when the pilot could?

Taking off from runway 9 with winds from 030—would we ordinarily expect the airplane to go off the runway to the left in such a crosswind?

Do you think the restricted window visibility was a distraction for the pilot?

We can't argue NTSB findings, but does anything else come to your mind that may have caused this accident?

MIA04CA005: During takeoff and when the pilot was about 1/4 of the distance from the end of the runway he attempted to pull back on the control yoke and lift off, but nothing happened. He noticed the airspeed was about 60 knots, but yet he could not raise the nose of the airplane, so he applied the brakes in an attempt to stop, and the airplane departed off the end of the runway. He did not remove the control lock prior to flight, and added that prior to the accident, there were no mechanical malfunctions.

Any pilot can make a mistake; this is a lesson in the redundancy built into our system to catch mistakes.

Did the pilot perform a preflight inspection?

Did the pilot use his checklist for "Controls Free and Correct"?

Do you think the pilot used ANY checklist carefully?

Why do you think that is? (complacency, feeling rushed)

CHI04CA095: The airplane sustained substantial damage when it exited the runway during an aborted landing. The instructor reported, "The aircraft turned final and flew a slightly low and fast approach to the runway. The aircraft touched down flat on the runway and because of the excess speed the aircraft bounced into the air a considerable amount. As the power was advanced for go-around, the aircraft began a left turn and drifted off the runway." At this point the instructor called for complete control of the aircraft and returned to wings level pitch attitude; however, despite the application of full power the aircraft refused to climb and touched down right main first on the grass to the north side of the runway. An examination of the wreckage revealed that the flight controls were correct and that engine controls were operational.

What is a stabilized approach?

The instructor talks about "the aircraft turned…" Who is responsible for what the airplane does?

What is "slightly low"? Is there ever an altitude in your mind that you are satisfied with "slightly low"?

Why did the airplane touchdown "flat?"

Why did the airplane turn left on the go-around?

ATL04CA129: Prior to departing on the return flight, the CFI checked Internet weather, and observed "bad weather" approaching the departure airport. He and the student departed from Runway 25 performing a soft-field takeoff. Immediately after rotation the CFI leveled the airplane to increase airspeed. The CFI stated "This took longer than usual due to wind shear." The airplane reached 60 knots and they were between 25 to 50 feet on initial takeoff climb, when they encountered a "severe crosswind gust of an estimated 40 to 50 knots from the right putting the wings in a near vertical attitude." The CFI applied rudder and aileron, and the airplane collided with the trees and the ground. Another pilot who landed at the airport before the accident airplane departed stated that black clouds were visible in the distance.

What does "black clouds" indicate to you?

What is the risk in rushing for takeoff ahead of "bad weather?"

How do you feel about the pilot's choice of a soft-field takeoff within this situation?

Aerodynamically, was there a better choice of takeoffs in consideration of "bad weather"?

Was the pilot over the runway centerline when the gust was encountered?

CHI02LA111: The air carrier passenger flight encountered severe turbulence while in cruise. Three passengers were seriously injured, while nine passengers and three flight attendants received minor injuries during the turbulence. The airplane was traveling at 37,000 feet altitude. Weather products showed extreme-intensity thunderstorms existed in the area. Weather data and aircraft position radar data show that the airplane was 9 miles S–SW of a cloud buildup that extended to 39,000 feet. Additionally, the airplane was 5 miles west of an extreme intensity radar echo associated with the thunderstorms in the area. No National Weather Service aviation weather advisories were in effect for the location and time of the turbulence encounter. Communications transcripts show that the flight crew requested and was granted a course deviation for weather about 10 minutes prior to the upset. However, the Digital Flight Data Recorder shows that the seat belt sign was illuminated only 10 seconds prior to the encounter.

Is a 39,000-foot thunderstorm robust? What would you expect for turbulence around this cell?

What is the risk of flying at an altitude near the top of the thunderstorm?

Okay, so you don't normally fly at 39,000 feet. But, aerodynamically, what is the implication of flying near the upper limits of any aircraft service ceiling in turbulence?

ANC04LA009: The flight was on an IAP in dark night conditions. The weather at the destination airport at the time of arrival was 2 miles visibility, in light snow, with an 800 foot obscured ceiling. LDA-2 approach MDA is 1,000 feet, and the distance from the FAF to the touchdown zone is 3.2 miles. The aircraft was cleared for the LDA-2 approach to Runway 8, and was inside the FAF when the aircraft hit a tree, but was able to continue flying. The pilot said the tree that was struck by the airplane was about 2 miles from the airport, and .24 miles north of the course centerline. The inspector said the tree's base elevation was between 200 to 300 feet MSL, and he estimated the tree's height at 100 feet AGL.

Would a clear night with a moon have helped the pilot see the tree? Would he have been looking?

What is an LDA? An LDA-2?

Do you suppose this was the best choice of IAPs? Did he consider others?

The MDA is 1,000—is that MSL or AGL? The ceiling is 800—is this MSL or AGL?

Is 800/2 within your personal flight minimums?

.24 miles off centerline, 2 miles away…how many dots on the CDI do you think he was off?

This is a lesson in CFIT.

Chapter 11

Gold Standards for Employees

"Corporate culture has a very real influence on the attitudes and performance of the people within an organization; there is no question in my mind that management decisions and actions, or more frequently, indecisions and inactions, cause accidents."

—John Lauber, NTSB

Flight School Culture

In the same way that scenario-based training helps develop judgment and decision making in pilots, it can instill good business judgment in employees of the flight school. For the flight school manager, incorporating scenario training into an employee-training program yields standardization. The flight school manager can be at ease knowing that in his absence, employees are making decisions with the same priorities and motivations.

The culture of the flight school must be such that pilots, dispatchers and other employees are involved and aware of pilots, aircraft, and situations that affect safety and business in general. At every level of the flight school, employees should understand how they contribute to the school's safety culture. Training is the key to building the right culture, providing employees with a vision of the desired performance standard.

A Gold Standards Approach to Training Instructors to Evaluate Crew Performance is a NASA Aviation Safety Program. The program attempts to teach new instructors how to train and evaluate pilot performance in the same way that experienced instructors do. The project establishes the skills and judgment of a company's most experienced instructor as a baseline for new instructors at that company. A Gold Standards approach can be used as a model to train any flight school employee, with the flight school manager as the baseline in decision making.

Gold standards in scenario-based training are especially important in two areas: front desk personnel, and check instructors. These are the most common areas where consistent and standardized decisions regarding the flight school business are required. This is especially true when the flight school manager is often away flying, and is not available to employees for consultation. The benefits for the school, its employees, and customers are the consistency in which business is conducted.

Front Desk Personnel Standardization Training Scenarios

At most flight schools, the front desk is the hub of communications and activities. Yet, large numbers of front desk personnel don't come to the business with an aviation background. Training them is important because they are the first to encounter customers, and if properly trained they can be a defensive line against potential safety breaches.

Specific standardization training in management expectations helps front desk personnel make smart business decisions while the manager is away. The following collection of scenarios and their alternative answers will open the door to discuss aviation business concepts with front desk personnel.

1. Mr. Ego does not see any benefit to aircraft checkout procedures and assumes they are an attempt by the school to milk money from his wallet. He is an airline transport pilot and expects that you will allow him access to aircraft keys based on his experience and seniority—after all, he routinely flies a much bigger plane than what the flight school has. The Chief and managers are not available. What will you do?

   A. Who does this guy think he is? Show Mr. Ego the written Standard Operating Procedures.

   B. Sympathize with Mr. Ego but inform him that all pilots participate in a checkout to receive rental privileges and schedule him with an instructor and airplane.

   C. Issue the keys to the plane. An airline transport pilot is the best of all pilots and he will be fine flying this little airplane.

2. Mr. Important has friends in high places. Because of his influence with many people, he plans to bring a great deal of new business to the school. However, today he would like to fly on account, stating that he will bring a check tomorrow. He has no credit cards. The Chief and managers are not available. What will you do?

A. Let Mr. Important fly without paying. Do not risk jeopardizing future new business by insulting a wealthy and well-connected man.

B. Show Mr. Important the written Standard Operating Procedures and plead with him not to ask you to do something that will get you into trouble with the Chief.

C. Let Mr. Important fly a less expensive plane—it seems to be a happy middle-ground.

3. Mr. Nice is purchasing navigational charts. One of his requested charts in the display case is obsolete. It is the last chart and he needs it. The Chief and managers are not available. What will you do?

A. Inform him that the chart is obsolete. Throw it in the trash. Do not give it to the pilot, he is not allowed to fly with an obsolete chart.

B. Inform him that the chart is obsolete and sell him the obsolete chart.

C. Inform him that the chart is obsolete and give him the obsolete chart, at no charge.

4. Ms. Lovely is asking you to schedule her for a progress check, but you notice that she has not flown in the previous 44 days. The Chief and managers are not available. What will you do?

A. Schedule the progress check, but confirm with an instructor that everything is okay.

B. Ask Ms. Lovely questions about her confidence and ability to perform maneuvers. Don't decide for her, but continue to ask questions until it occurs to her that the only correct and obvious decision is to schedule a flight lesson instead of a progress check.

C. Inform Ms. Lovely that her chances are poor that she'll pass the progress check after not having flown for 44 days. You will not schedule a progress check, but have an instructor return her call.

5. A herd of FAA inspectors—looking very stern and rigid—is standing in front of you, asking if the Chief is available. The Chief and other managers are in the facility, but engaged with customers. What will you do?

Continued on next page...

A. Say yes and go find him. If he is not
available, locate another manager.

B. If the FAA is here, it can't be a good thing.
Suggest they make an appointment and come
back at another time. The Chief is very busy.

C. Locate the Chief and inquire if he is available.
If not, handle their requests yourself.

6. The press and media personnel with cameras and microphones
are standing in front of you, asking questions about the school
and airport operations. The Chief and managers are not available.
What will you do?

A. Answer their questions sweetly, positively and with
a smile. This is great publicity for the school!

B. Don't try to handle this yourself. Call airport security.

C. Clam up. Don't say anything that you don't want to
see on the 6 o'clock news. Request that they leave.

7. Mr. Whiney has returned the keys to the rental aircraft you just
issued, stating that a tire is low and he does not want to fly it
that way. You know the tires are fine. The Chief and managers
are not available. What will you do?

A. Apologize for the inconvenience, thank him for catching
the problem, issue keys to another airplane and inform
him that we'll have maintenance check the tire.

B. Thank him for conducting a thorough preflight
inspection, but inform the customer that the tire
is fine. Find an instructor to go preflight with
him to teach him the correct tire pressure.

C. Call the maintenance department and
let them deal with Mr. Whiney.

8. You notice Big-Daddy, Big-Momma, Big-Son and Big-Daughter
piling a big heap of baggage into a little Cessna 172 in preparation
for a Big family vacation. Neither the Chief nor another manager
is available. What will you do?

A. This is no big problem. It's a four-place airplane. He
is a certificated pilot and knows what to do.

B. Inform an instructor or if one is not available, ask the
customer to delay takeoff until one becomes available.

C. Call the Air Traffic Control Tower and ask that the
plane not be given authorization to take off.

9. It is getting dark and time to go home. You find that you are
missing keys to an airplane. The scheduling system shows a

student on a solo cross-country that should have been back more than an hour ago. Neither the Chief nor another manager is available. What will you do?

    A. Attempt to reach the customer's cell phone, leave a message if he doesn't answer.

    B. Call the instructor that authorized the solo cross-country. Have him return to the airport.

    C. Call the airports listed on his flight plan to see if personnel there have seen the plane and if they serviced fuel into the plane. Leave a message for the pilot to call if he shows up.

    D. Call FSS. Don't delay, it's getting dark.

    E. All four, in that sequential order.

10. A thunderstorm is in full force and you notice an airplane's tiedown ropes break. The airplane is moving about and is at risk of hitting another plane on the flight line. No one else is available to help you. What will you do?

    A. Nothing. You could get hurt trying to handle an airplane in a thunderstorm.

    B. Take the keys, hop in the plane and attempt to drive it away from the remainder of the fleet.

    C. Try to maneuver the other at risk plane out of harm's way.

Check Instructor Standardization Training Scenarios

Check Instructors are those senior instructors in larger flight schools that administer flight evaluations, which are sometimes referred to as progress checks or stage checks. In schools that have more than a handful of instructors, the Chief normally delegates responsibility for school quality training standards to Check Instructors.

To be effective, the Check Instructor should make decisions pertaining to quality standards and training policies just as the Chief would. Standardization-training scenarios help the Chief create a "Mini-me" in the Check Instructor. With this in place, pilots and instructors can see that the school is evaluating performance with consistency. The following battery of scenarios presents discussion points for standardization in Check Instructors.

1. Mr. Important does not see any benefit to progress checks and assumes they are an attempt by the school to milk money from his wallet. You are working with him on the first progress check, but he is obviously in a foul mood and is not receptive to the ordeal. What will you do?

A. Show Mr. Important the progress checks printed in the syllabus book. Show him the FAA regulations regarding progress checks. Explain that the school is not milking his wallet, but doing what they know is right in making him a safe pilot. Assure him that he is a good pilot, that he should have no trouble completing the progress check quickly and you will make every effort to be efficient with his time.

B. Sympathize with Mr. Important but inform him that he must participate in a progress check. He will not be allowed to continue with flight training until he has passed a progress check.

C. Send Mr. Important to the Chief and let him deal with the issue.

2. Ms. Lovely is on your schedule for the pre-solo progress check, but reviewing the training record with her, you find that she has not flown in the previous 44 days. What will you do?

A. If the instructor has scheduled a progress check for Ms. Lovely then you should assume that she is prepared and ready for the check. Do the progress check and evaluate her performance accordingly.

B. Ask Ms. Lovely questions about her confidence and ability to perform the listed maneuvers. Don't decide for her, but continue to ask questions until it occurs to her that the only correct and obvious decision is to turn this flight into a lesson instead of a progress check. You were smart and set up an instructor ahead of time to fly with her, knowing you would not be eligible to conduct her progress check for another 3 flight hours.

C. Inform Ms. Lovely that the chance of her passing the progress check after having not flown for 44 days is poor. You have authorization from the Chief to turn this appointment into the next normal lesson for her.

3. Ms. Priss is your favorite customer. She is a successful business person; charming and intelligent, but you suspect she has poor study habits. You see from her training record that she has required three attempts on Block Quiz 1 and 2 before passing with the minimum score. She has six hours and is on your schedule for the first progress check. What will you do?

A. Conduct the progress check. Assume that Ms. Priss knows she needs to study better and does not need you to treat her like a schoolgirl. However, mention your concern to the instructor and let him handle it.

B. Conduct the progress check. Inform the Chief about the poor instructional performance and suggest a meeting to reinforce the staff's awareness of the Block Quiz pass rate.

C. Conduct the progress check. During the debrief, affirm her abilities and intelligence. Nurture the standards by stressing the importance of learning the information. Help her identify good study habits.

4. You requested a steep turn to the left. Mr. Big did a steep turn to the right. But more than that, he was constantly +100 feet followed by an immediate -100 feet. The constant porpoising is really annoying. What will you do?

A. Mr. Big did not perform the maneuver you requested. He does not pass the evaluation on this maneuver even though his performance was within altitude deviation standards. You may however, give him a second chance at performing the maneuver.

B. You are a wise instructor and correctly recognize a typical mistake in left/right. No problem. The maneuver is within standards so Mr. Big will pass today. However, as part of your debrief, nurture the standards by reinforcing smooth control inputs and attitude flying.

C. Mr. Big did not perform the maneuver you requested. He does not pass the evaluation on this maneuver.

5. Mr. Senior Instructor is very upset that you failed his student on a progress check and insists that Mr. Student is a good pilot and deserves to have passed. Mr. Senior Instructor is insisting on a conference with you that you feel will become confrontational. How will you handle it?

A. You know that supervising or counseling the CFI staff is not within your job scope. Invite/encourage/beg/insist the Chief to sit in on the conference.

B. You conference with Mr. Senior Instructor and inform him how you were trained to do your job and the standards that are required to pass the progress check.

C. You decline the meeting with Mr. Senior Instructor. He has not been trained to conduct progress checks and is in no position to tell you how to do your job. The company chose you for a reason, not him, to conduct progress checks.

6. During a routine progress check, Pablo is very vocal about one instructor being a stupid bum who never meets his appointments on time and has a careless attitude in the plane. But Pablo won't give you the bad instructor's name for fear of getting him into trouble. What will you do?

   A. Don't press Pablo when it's so easy to look at the training record to see whom he's been flying with. Respect Pablo's privacy. Thank him for this tidbit; it will be more difficult to identify the CFI without Pablo's information, but you will try. Inform the Chief and let him handle it.

   B. Encourage Pablo to give up his confidential information. The flight school must know who this instructor is and correct his attitude and habits. Inform the Chief and let her handle it.

   C. If Pablo doesn't wish to discuss it, then it obviously is not as bad as you think it is. Don't worry about it. When Pablo is ready, he will be forthcoming with the information and it can be dealt with then.

7. Veronica is beautiful and blonde. You have told her that she needs additional work with an instructor before moving forward with new training. She responds with subtle but obviously frisky advances, tempting you with favors in exchange for a passing grade. What will you do?

   A. Trick her into thinking that you will pass her to take advantage of her favors. But then make an excuse for why you can't pass her and schedule a recheck.

   B. Be strong. Tell Veronica that it is not in her best interest to pass today. It's important that she learns to safely control the aircraft. Show faith in her ability to get the job done with just a little more instruction.

   C. Pass her. After all, she will be reviewing all those maneuvers again in upcoming lessons. You can recheck the items found deficient in a follow-up progress check.

8. Ms. Sweet is on her second attempt at the Solo Cross-Country Progress Check. You know something she doesn't. You know that her intended heading was 030, but have witnessed her flying a perfect 300-degree heading for the past 20 minutes. What will you do?

   A. Stop the progress check. Ms. Sweet was not able to perform the task to standards so you may not pass her. Return her to the instructor for more training and schedule a recheck.

B. Encourage Ms. Sweet to use all cockpit resources, including the autopilot, to reduce her workload. If she is not on her way to being on course soon after, say something like, "Show me with your finger on the chart where we are" to verify the unknown position. Then say "This isn't going well, let's continue with the other maneuvers and we'll finish the cross-country another day."

C. Tell Ms. Sweet of her error. Help her to plan an intercept to her course and resume the progress check from that point. If all goes well, she could still pass.

Exercise

1. Suppose you are the flight school manager faced with the task of developing an employee training plan. Start with clear ideas about the types of situations flight school employees may encounter that could put the business at risk of either customer dissatisfaction or breaches of safety. Then articulate the decisions that you would make if you were available for consultation during the situation. Give as alternative answers in the scenario limits for when your best decision may or may not be appropriate. Of course, your ability to develop a quality plan will depend on your previous experiences in similar situations.

Chapter 12

Designing Your Own Scenarios

Scenario Ingredients

For seasoned instructors, designing scenarios is second nature. The seasoned instructor has been teaching with scenarios for years, he just didn't realize it. For others, a few pointers may be helpful. This chapter will make sure that all important ingredients are included.

Ideas for Great Scenarios
- Use the details from a recent flight and turn it into a scenario.
- Replay your favorite flying story, turning it into a scenario. Simply turn "this happened to me" into "if this happened to you, what you would do?"
- Look for the "I Learned About Flying from That" (*Flying*) or "Never Again" (*AOPA Pilot*) type of articles in magazines and turn them into scenarios.
- Use NTSB and NASA ASRS reports.

The Execution
- Prepare. Prepare. Prepare.
- Pretend you are going on a real flight, even if it is simulated.
- Use actual charts, real weather and POH performance for your training airplane.
- Make it fun. Play the game. Get into the role.
- For excellent, high-performing pilots, don't cut the sessions short but keep raising the bar by nudging up performance standards.

The Rules
1. Make it realistic. The design should include preflight activities with details pertaining to flight planning, paperwork, and the Pilot's Operating Handbook. It should be conducted with proper, formal phraseology during radio communications.

2. Bring in issues that involve several disciplines (weather, regulations, terrain, etc.).

3. Design a scenario to illustrate a specific point, and apply knowledge in a practical situation.

4. Don't include simultaneous equipment failures or near-death situations. Don't string back-to-back, unrelated situations. They are not realistic and do not enhance the pilot's requirement to make decisions.

5. For maximum effectiveness, the scenario should allow pilot decision-making. Look for opportunities in the scenario for the pilot to make decisions.

6. Don't overload the pilot. A misconception is that cockpit failures and weather issues should be stacked up until the pilot is overloaded. Fill the scenario with routine, simple opportunities for decision making. Good scenarios are straightforward and simple.[1]

7. Allow a variety of outcomes depending on the decisions made by the pilot. The scenario will evolve into a situation totally built by the pilot's decisions. The pilot must deal with whatever problem he sees until the situation is either resolved or the airplane (simulator) is back on the ground.

8. Scenarios should include the importance of preflight and taxi. Of 125 ASRS incident reports reviewed, 90% of all human errors occurred in the preflight or taxi-out phase of operation. See "Errors Made by Pilots," Figure 12-1.[2]

9. Scenarios should not be long cross-countries. In fact, in weather-related accidents, the majority occurred inside 98 kilometers (50 NM) of departure. The influence of the halfway point on pilot behavior is significant. The majority of occurrences happen in the last half of the flight. Scenarios should strive to put the pilot beyond the halfway milestone.[3]

10. Adequately prepare the pilot for success. Inform the pilot of any details needed to plan and execute the flight successfully. This might include such things as the objective of what the pilot can expect to learn or experience, the planned destination(s), weather, and aircraft. It could also include the flight plan, initial clearance or other facts the pilot isn't expected to include in his initial planning. Inform the pilot of the materials and cockpit tools he should bring to the scenario such as charts, headset, timer, kneeboard, etc. A pilot who is surprised with an obviously forgotten tool will feel as though treated unfairly if the flight

doesn't go as well as hoped. Include the approximate time the scenario is expected to require.

11. Scenarios should foster open communication. They should encourage active participation during the debriefing. Share best practices or known instances of consistent achievement of the desired outcomes. Create strategies expected to lead to successful outcomes. Don't trick pilots or intentionally set them up for undesirable outcomes. Establish descriptions of successful and unsuccessful performance.

12. Design one scenario and use it. Learn from pilots what they find effective in the training airplane or ATD. Good scenarios take time to construct and test. Lessons learned from the first scenario will ensure that the instructor has the recipe correct before attempting others.

13. Scenarios must have a purpose and consequences. Adults learn better when they relate what is being accomplished to that which is real. Be creative. For a navigation or instrument approach lesson, the pilot is going to pick up his mother at one airport and then go to your sister's wedding at another airport. A ground reference maneuvers lesson might be a photo mission or search and rescue. What does the pilot do with the pressure of getting your mother to a wedding? Or with a photographer threatening never to use your company again if the pilot does not fly lower than 500 feet?

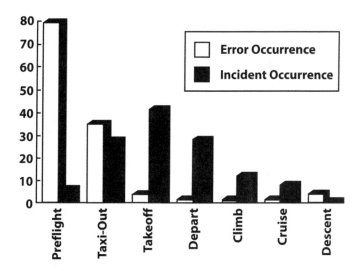

Figure 12-1. Errors made by pilots.

Scenario Storyboard: Daytona Beach to Washington, DC

Decision Opportunity: Planning

- ❏ PIC is owner of C182 (MFD/Datalink Weather/Traffic)
- ❏ Departing Daytona Beach, FL
  - Sunday evening with two business associates.
  - One is a 140-pound pilot-friend.
  - One is his 240-pound friend you've not met before.
- ❏ All three have a meeting at FAA HQ Monday 8:00 A.M.
- ❏ VFR at Daytona Beach, MVFR Washington with MVFR en route
- ❏ Weather Information
  - METAR at departure 251700Z 27010KT 10SM CLR 12/7 A2995 RMK A01
  - TAF for departure 251800Z 251818 2505KT 10SM FEW 0500
  - METAR for destination 251700Z 3105KT 3SM BKN 020 00/M14 A2990
  - TAF for destination 251800Z 251818 3305KT 3SM BKN 020
- ❏ Area Forecast—Occasional light turbulence, negative icing, improving ceilings and visibilities as a cold front moves out.

The "5P's" Check

- ❏ The Plan
  - Direct or airways
  - Nonstop or two-stop
  - How much fuel? Are we legal? (Instructor will add fuel as requested up to weight and balance limits)
  - Night/overwater/mountains/IFR — am I concerned?? (Is this an accident chain?)
- ❏ The Plane
  - Maintenance status
- ❏ The Pilot
  - How early did I get up? How tired am I? (IMSAFE)
  - Am I current? When was my last flight in any "real" weather? When was my last IFR flight? How long has it been since I've been in clouds? When was my last night flight?
- ❏ The Passengers
  - One private pilot and one non-pilot: Who sits where?
  - Duties, familiarity with IFR charts, equipment

- Urgency of trip (employment relationship)
- Passenger safety briefing includes "We may have to stop short and drive"

❏ The Programming
- Can we use the GPS with an outdated database?
- What do we need to fly?

Decision Opportunity: Pretakeoff

❏ Engine shows 1 quart lower than expected.
❏ Pilot-friend asks to carry an additional 100 pounds of computer equipment.
❏ Clearance delivery gives you an IFR ATC ground hold for 10 minutes.
❏ Landing light is inoperative.
❏ Nonpilot passenger is fidgety and makes several trips to the restroom.

Ask Yourself:

❏ What are the risk factors? Have they changed?
❏ What do we know that will help?
❏ What don't we know that may help?
❏ What can we do to improve our situation?
❏ Continue, divert or abort?

Decision Opportunity: One hour after takeoff

❑ In clear at 9,000 MSL.

❑ Tops are at 8,000 MSL.

❑ FSS: Departure Special Weather: 500-2 at 2045Z
       Destination Weather: 1500-3 at 2007Z

❑ 737 is holding over VOR

❑ Oil temp is down 3 degrees.

❑ Oil pressure is up 2 pounds.

❑ JAX Center—new routing: Direct-to Destination

The "5P's" Check

❑ The Plan
  • Fuel status?
  • Are we thinking ahead?

❑ The Plane
  • What's the temp at 9,000 feet?

❑ The Pilot
  • Tired? What time is it now?

❑ The Passengers
  • Bathroom problem? Sick?

❑ The Programming

  • Entire route and approach to destination

Decision Opportunity: Two hours after takeoff

❑ Ground speed down 10 knots from planned.

❑ ATC assigns new route clearance V373 GSO V266 SBV Flight
     Planned Route

❑ ATC requests an altitude change. Your choice of 7,000 feet or
     11,000 feet. Temp at 7,000 feet is 4°C and temp at 11,000 feet
     is 1°C.

❑ Winds aloft at 11,000 – headwind of 10 kts and at 7,000 –
     headwind of 20 kts

Ask Yourself:

  ❑ What are the risk factors? Have they changed?
  ❑ What do we know that will help?

❑ What don't we know that may help?

❑ What can we do to improve our situation?

❑ Continue, divert or abort?

Decision Opportunity: Descent

❏ IAD Center reports a radar outage (that's why the 737 was holding!), asks you to report the next intersection. Can you make a proper position report?

❏ Backseat passenger repeatedly asks "Are we there yet?"

❏ Oil pressure up one more pound and temp down 2 degrees.

❏ The autopilot is having real trouble maintaining wings level and appears unstable in pitch.

❏ It's dark outside. You are in and out of the clouds.

❏ ATC requests reporting over STAR intersection for approach into destination.

❏ ATIS report active runway is 19L, expect vectors to the ILS and sequencing around heavy jet traffic. (You will be flying further around to the north side of the airport at Washington, DC).

❏ Ice forming on the windshield.

❏ Oil pressure is up 2 more pounds and oil temp is down 5 degrees.

Ask Yourself:

❏ What are the risk factors? Have they changed?

❏ What do we know that will help?

❏ What don't we know that may help?

❏ What can we do to improve our situation?

❏ Continue, divert or abort?

The "5P's" Check

❏ The Plan
  • Fuel status with re-route?
  • ATIS: Which approach is in use? WX minimums?
  • Consider alternate?

❏ The Plane
  • Temp? Icing?

❏ The Pilot
  • Am I safe under these conditions?

❏ The Passengers
  • Is backseat passenger sick?
  • Do I reassure him or fly the airplane?
  • How can the passengers help?

❏ The Programming
  • What do you plan to fly/routing/approach?

- What time is it? Do I have to check the fixes in the GPS or do I fly off the current paper charts?

Decision Opportunity: Beginning Approach

❏ ATC radar back in service.

❏ "Expect vectors to runway 19R, you are number four for the runway behind heavy jet traffic, what speed can you maintain on final?

❏ Autopilot is very sloppy now and seems unable to maintain heading or altitude.

❏ Airspeed has dropped 20 knots.

The "5P's" Check

❏ The Plan
  - Your fuel reserve is below 30 minutes now.
  - Divert, minimum fuel, or emergency fuel.

❏ The Plane
  - Think of descent temps/icing?

❏ The Pilot
  - Feel comfortable as single pilot in these WX conditions?
  - Fatigued?
  - Checklist done?

❏ The Passengers
  - How can they help?
  - How can you reassure them? Keep them busy?
  - Should you divert to Richmond and drive the rest of the way?

❏ The Programming
  - Hand-fly the approach?
  - Have you thought of all alternatives with a runway change?
  - Is there holding in progress until the runways open up? Fuel?
  - Do you have a back-up route programmed just in case?
  - Which is better, set the navaids then program the route, or vice versa?

Decision Opportunity: Continuing the Approach

❏ ATC loses radar again.

❏ ATC assigns you a full VOR approach to another runway.

❏ After established outbound on the VOR approach, you recheck fuel.

❏ Passenger tells you they really need to use the bathroom.

❏ More ice on leading edge of wings.

❏ Where do you land?

The "5P's" Check

❑ The Plan
  • What are the risk factors now?
❑ The Plane
  • Icing? What can you do to keep her in the air?
❑ The Pilot
  • Up to the challenge of a non-precision approach in solid IFR?
  • Checklists done? What are you focusing on?
❑ The Passengers
  • Are passengers okay with diverting and driving? Does it matter?
❑ The Programming
  • At destination, have two approaches programmed.
  • Do you understand the weather conditions?

Conclusion

Designing an effective scenario is simple to do and there are many sources for helpful information. In this chapter and in the chapters that precede it, many good examples and clues have been given for designing an effective scenario.

Exercise

1. Write a scenario for your local area, your training airplane and your airspace using the storyline from a recent magazine article.

Chapter 13

Why Bother Using Scenarios to Train Pilots?

"The significant problems we have cannot be solved at the same level of thinking with which they were created."
—*Albert Einstein*

Benefits to Instructors and Industry

Scenario-based training requires diligence, creativity and organization by the flight instructor. It's difficult for instructors to gain momentum in scenario-based training when nothing in their training has prepared them for it. So, many instructors at this point may be asking, "why bother?"

There are specific benefits for the instructor. Scenario-based training is the easiest way to brand training, making the instructor who uses it unique and improved over others. Even without additional FAA approvals, it's clear to the customer that "modern teaching methods" are different. This can be featured in marketing efforts and in attracting additional clientele. When the instructional service is of higher value, it's justifiable for the hourly rate charged to the customer to reflect that. Training sessions typically last longer, thus billable hours are higher for the instructor; but there are fewer sessions, thus there is no additional overall cost to the customer.

However, this chapter focuses on three primary benefits of scenario-based training for the industry. Instructors must go the extra mile because:

1. Pilot error will never be eliminated. Pilots must be taught to manage errors.
2. Technology alone will not make flying safer. Pilots have a preset tolerance for risk and must be motivated toward safer behaviors.

4. Long-term, career instructors have had specific success in graduating safe pilots by instilling a safety culture in their local areas. Scenario-based training is their tool of choice in producing a culture of safety.

Pilot Error

Dr. R. Key Dismukes is the chief scientist for Human Factors at NASA's Ames Research Center. In a 2000 panel session focused on Crew Error, Dr. Dismukes summarized the discussions:[1]

"The majority of accidents are attributed to [pilot] crew error. I argue that this well-known fact is widely misinterpreted, even by experts in aviation safety. Certainly, if pilots never made mistakes the accident rate would go down dramatically, but is it reasonable to expect pilots not to make mistakes?

Fallacy: Error can be eliminated if pilots are sufficiently vigilant and conscientious. The truth is that vigilant, conscientious pilots make mistakes, even in tasks at which they are highly skilled.

Fallacy: The crew was deficient if some aspect of their performance contributed to an accident, even if the vast majority of their performance was adequate or better. The truth is that error is probabilistic and can never be eliminated completely."

The panel discussion was concerned primarily with airline operations; however, the issues can be applied to general aviation. One way Dr. Dismukes suggests to improve safety is to "stop thinking of pilot errors as the prime cause of accidents, but rather think of errors as the consequence of many factors that combine to create the conditions for accidents."

Good scenario-based training does exactly that.

Risk Homeostatis Theory

A theory called Risk Homeostatis Theory (RHT) is best illustrated by the quote "Give me a ladder that is twice as stable, and I will climb it twice as high. But give me a cause for caution, and I'll be twice as shy."[2] It portrays how people change behavior in response to the addition of an added safety device.

One notion of RHT is that people have a certain level of risk they choose to accept and, if given additional safety equipment to make a task safer, they engage in riskier behavior, so that overall the level of risk of an activity remains the same. The best studied examples involve automobiles: taxicabs in Germany equipped with anti-lock brake systems were not involved in fewer accidents than taxis without these brakes, and they were driven in a more careless manner. Habitual non-users of seat belts who were made to buckle up increased their moving speed and decreased their following distance. Thus they engaged in riskier behavior.[3]

RHT relates to pilots as well. In the 1970s the Piper Aircraft Company equipped retractable-gear aircraft with a throttle horn. Assuming that if the pilot retarded the throttle as the aircraft was preparing to land, the horn sounded, reminding the pilot to lower the landing gear. Yet, pilots routinely pulled the circuit breaker and flew with the safety horn silenced.[4]

Another notion of RHT is that accidents can't be reduced with a "technological fix." Instead, accidents are only reduced with programs that enhance safer human behavior. The riskiness of the way people behave will not change unless the amount of risk they are willing to incur is reduced.

A TV commercial showed a new Volvo spraying a whirlwind of snow as it sped up an alpine road, snaking around wicked curves on the edge of a rocky cliff. The announcer proclaimed, "With Volvo's four-wheel drive you can dance through the snow gracefully."[5] The commercial gave viewers permission to engage in riskier driving as a result of having four-wheel drive equipment.

RHT points out how important it is for instructors to promote safe habits and instill pilots with motivation to fly with wider safety margins. Pilots and flight instructors who are aware of RHT are better equipped to understand that we each already possess the best safety gear available—our brains.

Ten Habits of Highly Experienced Instructors

Safety is the most desired consequence of flight training. Every flight instructor can agree that safety is paramount and everyone wants to be safe. How can an instructor ensure the safety of flight training activities? How can instructors train pilots who will fly with a safety mindset after graduating the protected training environment?

A recent survey of 14 seasoned instructors revealed the common characteristics in their training methodology.[6] The characteristics of seasoned instructors are listed below. They could be the Gold Standards for our industry. Nearly every survey-instructor follows the conventions promoted in this book in that they practice and preach:

1. Decision making and situational awareness
2. The major concern during training has little to do with passing checkrides or exams
3. The use of training scenarios and exercises
4. Precise aircraft control
5. Strong cross-country training and the "sub-skills" it requires
6. Fundamental navigation skills: dead reckoning and pilotage
7. Stabilized approaches
8. Emergency training and emergency "mental preparedness"
9. Spin training—not just awareness
10. Flying in the weather

Conclusions

This book describes real examples in scenario-based training methodology to train good pilots. It provides credible, recent scientific research in support of its examples and gives flight instructors the tools to populate our industry with safe and responsible aviation citizens. Flight instructors can accomplish this by emulating the Gold Standards that seasoned instructors use during flight training.

Exercise

1. Interview five active, career flight instructors and discuss in a paper the Gold Standards that you wish to emulate.

Epilogue

    Aero-Tech, the flight school where I am Chief Instructor, had two training facilities for a period of five years. One was located in Lexington, Kentucky and the other, 50 miles west in Louisville, Kentucky. I work from the Lexington location and admit to carrying out my personal experiments in teaching methods on the instructors and pilots there. As a result, the Lexington campus has made full use of the scenarios and exercises described. The two facilities saw different results in pilot training.

    Far from a scientific survey, the results were enough for staff to give a hearty thumbs-up to continued use and expansion of use for scenarios in all aspects of flight training including Sport Pilot through Airline Transport Pilot training, flight reviews and aircraft checkouts. The school does not have a FITS-accepted training program for any initial certification program, but has folded FITS philosophies into generic, commercially-available syllabi. Here's what was reported:

    Lexington is located in Charlie Airspace. The Lexington facility (scenario training) graduated private pilot candidates with an average of 47.5 total flight hours. Pilots engaged in training activities on average 2.6 times each week and flew on average 6.0 hours per week.

    Louisville is located in Delta Airspace, underlying Charlie. The Louisville facility (traditional training) graduated private pilot candidates with an average of 60 total flight hours. Pilots engaged in training activities on average 1.1 times each week and flew on average .9 hours per week.

    Pilots were not required to complete any amount of training during a week at either location. In fact, they scheduled themselves with an online scheduling system. Pilots train in a wide range of aircraft including light sport aircraft, C-152/172, and technically-advanced aircraft with the G-1000.

Economic benefits to customers through reduced flight hours could be enough to justify training based on scenarios, but there is more—Lexington pilots reported greater satisfaction in flight training. They reported feeling "trusted with flying." One pilot recalled, "Now when my wife asks where did you fly today, I have an answer with a destination."

Pilots with training from other flight schools, who transferred into a finish-up program, felt that scenario based training "put the fun back into training." A large percentage of pilots continue with additional training. Many return immediately, continuing in instrument training without a break. Many purchase an airplane, representing their commitment to long-term aviation goals.

When a school has pilots who are happy, flying regularly and making good progress, the instructors are happy. The instructors enjoyed teaching in scenarios. They reported higher morale and higher earnings. The Lexington facility retains flight instructors longer, on average for about 24 months.

But most important, since the school's inception in 1971, students and instructors in Lexington have enjoyed a safety record that far exceeds industry standards.[1]

Appendix

Contents

Radio-Call Pilot Aid
For normal VFR student operations at KLEX

INBOUND ARRIVAL

LEXINGTON ATIS 126.30

Info	Wind	Visibility	Sky	Temp	Altimeter	Runway

LEXINGTON APPROACH 120.15 (SOUTH)   120.75 (NORTH)

Pilot says: Lexington Approach, Cessna _____
Wait for an answer.
Pilots says: Cessna _____ is _____ miles _____ (N, S, E, W) at _____ feet, landing LEX with ATIS Information _____

Controller Says: Cessna _____ Squawk _____

Pilot Says: Cessna _____, squawk _____

Controller Says: Cessna _____ Radar Contact, (position) maintain _____ feet, fly heading _____

Pilot Says: _____ (N-Number)
Controller will instruct you when to change frequency.

LEXINGTON TOWER 119.1

Pilot Says: Lexington Tower, Cessna _____ inbound landing, runway _____

Controller Says: Cessna _____, runway _____
- [ ] Cleared to land
- [ ] Number _____ following _____
- [ ] Fly heading _____, Continue

Pilot says: _____ (N-Number)
Change frequency after clearing the runway and stopped.

LEXINGTON GROUND 121.9

Pilot Says: Ground, Cessna _____ clear of the active, taxi to the ramp...

Controller Says: Cessna _____
- [ ] Taxi to the ramp
- [ ] Hold short

Pilot says: _____ (N-Number) hold short / position&hold / runway crossing

---

OUTBOUND DEPARTURE

LEXINGTON ATIS 126.30

Info	Wind	Visibility	Sky	Temp	Altimeter	Runway

LEXINGTON GROUND 121.9

Pilot says: Lexington Ground, Cessna _____
Wait for an answer.
Pilots says: Cessna _____ at _____ feet, ready to taxi with ATIS Information _____

Controller Says: Cessna _____, maintain _____ feet, departure frequency on 120._____, squawk _____
- [ ] Taxi to runway _____
- [ ] Taxi to runway _____, hold short _____
- [ ] Hold Short _____

Pilot Says: _____ (N-Number) hold short / position&hold / runway crossing
Change frequency when ready to takeoff.

LEXINGTON TOWER 119.1

Pilot Says: Lexington Tower, Cessna _____ ready for takeoff runway _____

Controller Says: Cessna _____, runway _____
- [ ] Cleared for takeoff
- [ ] Taxi into position and hold
- [ ] Hold Short

Pilot says: _____ (N-Number) hold short / position&hold / runway crossing
Controller will instruct you when to change frequency.

LEXINGTON DEPARTURE 120.15 (SOUTH)   120.75 (NORTH)

Pilot Says: Departure, Cessna _____ with you at _____ feet.

Controller Says: Cessna _____ radar contact,
- [ ] On course, climb to requested altitude
- [ ] Fly heading _____ climb to requested altitude

Pilot says: _____ (N-Number)
Pilot may request radar termination and frequency change after 10 miles.

Scenario 1

Scenario 2

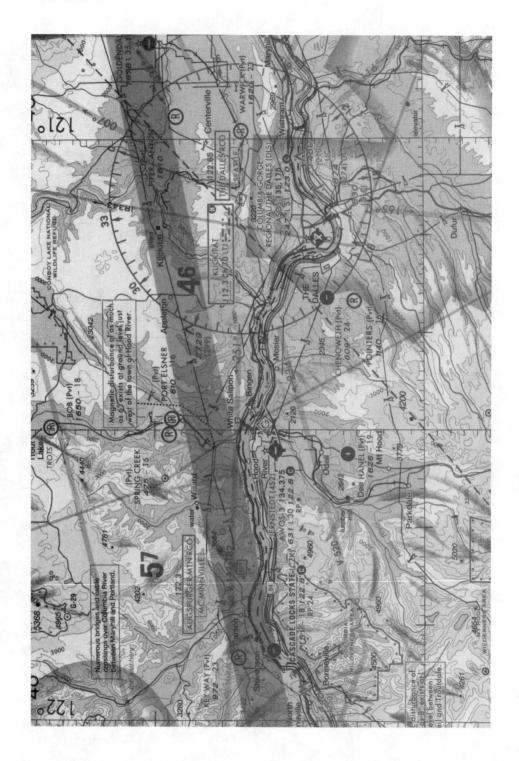

Scenario 3

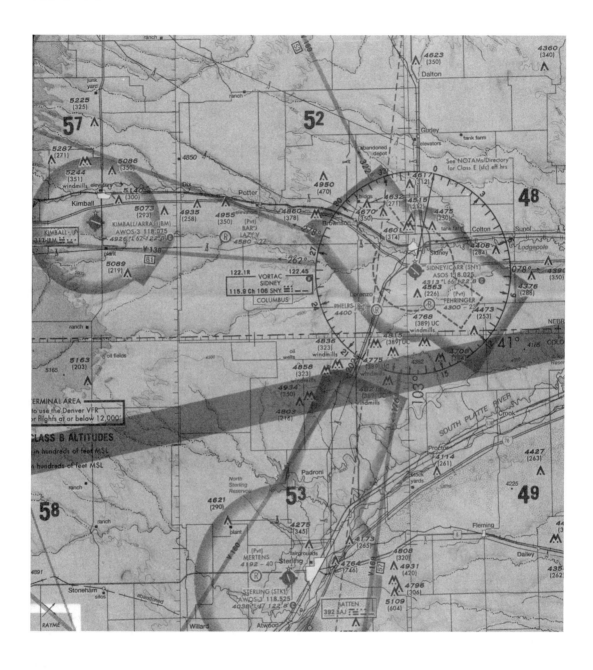

Scenario 4

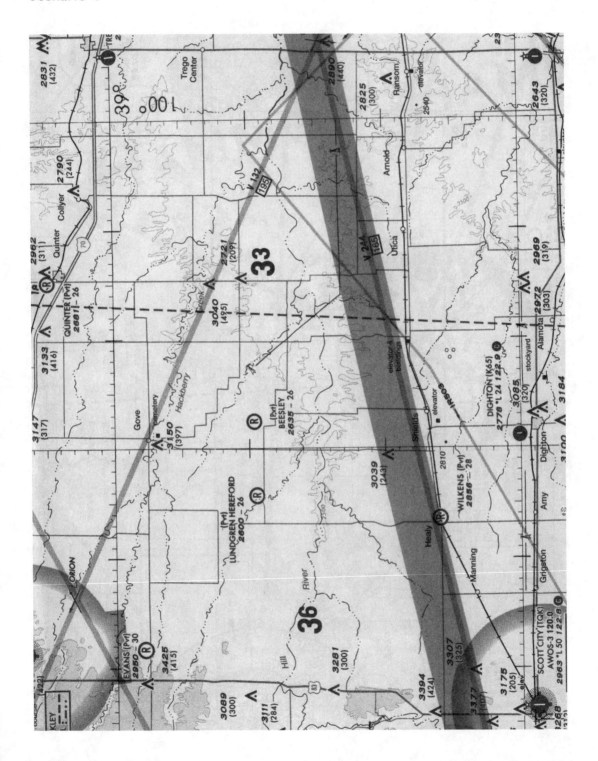

Learning Plateau Game Sheet

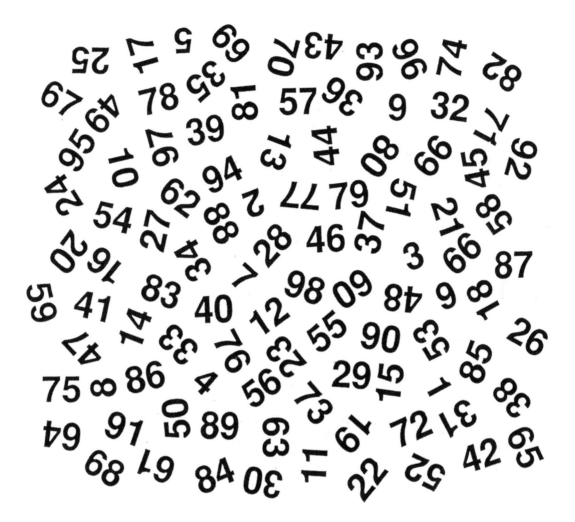

Glossary

aeronautical decision making (ADM). A systematic approach to the mental process used by aircraft pilots to consistently determine the best course of action in response to a given set of circumstances.

application. A basic level of learning where the student puts something to use that has been learned and understood.

automation bias. The relative willingness of the pilot to trust and use automated systems.

automation competence. The demonstrated ability to understand and operate the automated systems installed in the aircraft.

automation management. The demonstrated ability to control and navigate an aircraft by means of the automated systems installed in the aircraft.

critical safety tasks/event. Those mission-related tasks/events that if not accomplished quickly and accurately may result in damage to the aircraft or loss of life.

controlled flight into terrain (CFIT). An accident that occurs when an airworthy aircraft, under the control of a pilot, is flown into terrain (water or obstacles) with inadequate awareness on the part of the pilot of the impending disaster.

correlation. A basic level of learning where the student can associate what has been learned, understood, and applied with previous or subsequent learning.

course of training. A complete series of studies leading to attainment of a specific goal, such as a certificate of completion, graduation, or an academic degree.

Data Link Situational Awareness Systems. Systems that feed real-time information to the cockpit on weather, traffic, terrain and flight planning. This information may be displayed on the PFD, MFD or on other related cockpit displays.

demonstration–performance method. An educational presentation where an instructor FAA monitored currency program designed to assess and update a pilot's knowledge and skills.

evaluation. A system of critical thinking and skill evaluations designed to assess a training candidate's readiness to begin training at the required level.

FAA/Industry Training Standards (FITS). A new approach to GA flight training, one that embraces concepts central to system safety. These include risk management, aeronautical decision-making, situational awareness, and single-pilot resource management. Instead of treating each element as a separate or stand-alone lesson, scenario-based training will be used to efficiently integrate these important concepts into every instructional exercise.

flight training device (FTD). A full-size replica of the instruments, equipment, panels, and controls of an aircraft, or set of aircraft, in an open flight deck area or in an enclosed cockpit. A force (motion) cueing system or visual system is not required.

headwork. Required to accomplish a conscious, rational thought process when making decisions. Good decision-making involves risk identification and assessment, information processing, and problem solving.

hindsight bias. The inclination to see past events as being predictable and reasonable to expect. Evaluating an event based on what has happened rather than evaluating the likelihood of its happening in the future.

human factors. A multidisciplinary field devoted to optimizing human performance and reducing human error. It incorporates the methods and principles of the behavioral and social sciences, engineering, and physiology. It may be described as the applied science which studies people working together in concert with machines. Human factors involve variables that influence individual performance, as well as team or crew performance.

judgment. The mental process of recognizing and analyzing all pertinent information in a particular situation, a rational evaluation of alternative actions in response to it, and a timely decision on which action to take.

insight. The grouping of perceptions into meaningful wholes. Creating insight is one of the instructor's major responsibilities.

instrument proficiency check. An evaluation ride based on the instrument rating practical test standard, which is required to regain instrument flying privileges when the privileges have expired due to lack of currency.

learner centered grading. The object of scenario-based training is a change in the thought processes, habits, and behaviors of the students during the planning and execution of each scenario. Since the training is student-centered, success is measured in the following desired student outcomes: Students will be able to describe, explain, practice, perform, and manage/decide all aspects of the scenario effectively.

learning. A change in behavior as a result of experience.

learning plateau. A learning phenomenon where progress appears to cease or slow down for a significant period of time before once

lesson plan. An organized outline for a single instructional period. It is a necessary guide for the instructor in that it tells what to do, in what order to do it, and what procedure to use in teaching the material of a lesson.

Line Oriented Flight Training (LOFT). A form of training that uses full-mission stimulation.

Line Oriented Simulation (LOS). A modified form of LOFT. A form of training that involves only segmented parts of a LOFT scenario. LOS is frequently used for training in special situations and to avoid long unproductive simulated periods at cruise.

mission. Those tasks required for the safe and effective accomplishment of the mission(s) that the aircraft is capable of and required to conduct.

Multi-Function Display (MFD). Any display that combines primarily navigation, systems and situational awareness information onto a single electronic display.

Practical Test Standards (PTS). An FAA published list of standards which must be met for the issuance of a particular pilot certificate or rating. FAA inspectors and designated pilot examiners use these standards when conducting pilot practical tests and flight instructors should use the PTS while preparing applicants for practical tests.

Primary Flight Display (PFD). Any display that combines the primary six flight instruments plus other related performance, navigation and situational awareness information into a single electronic display.

poor judgment chain. A series of mistakes that may lead to an accident or incident. Two basic principles generally associated with the creation of a poor judgment chain are: 1) one bad decision often leads to another; and 2) as a string of bad decisions grows, it reduces the number of subsequent alternatives for continued safe flight. Aeronautical Decision Making is intended to break the poor judgment chain before it can cause an accident or incident.

risk management. The part of the decision making process which relies on situational awareness, problem recognition, and good judgment to reduce risks associated with each flight.

rote learning. A basic level of learning where the student has the ability to repeat back something learned, with no understanding or who composes and transmits a message made up of symbols, which are meaningful to listeners and readers.

scenario based training (SBT). A training system that uses a highly structured script of real-world experiences to address flight training objectives in an operational environment. Such training can include initial training, transition training, upgrade training, recurrent training and special training.

single-pilot resource management (SRM). The process of managing resources available to the single pilot. These would include the pilot's resource of preflight planning, personal knowledge, materials and personnel on board the aircraft, and additional resources beyond the cockpit.

situational awareness. The accurate perception and understanding of all the factors and conditions within the four fundamental risk elements that affect safety before, during, and after the flight.

system safety. The application of special technical and managerial skills to identify, analyze, assess, and control hazards and risks associated with a complete system (i.e., a typical flight). System safety is applied throughout the system's entire lifecycle (i.e., preflight planning to tie down) to achieve an acceptable level of risk within the constraints of operational effectiveness, time, and cost.

technically advanced aircraft (TAA). A general aviation aircraft that combines some or all of the following design features: advanced cockpit automation system (moving map GPS/glass cockpit) for IFR/VFR flight operations, automated engine and systems management, and integrated auto flight/autopilot systems.

training syllabus. A step-by-step, building block progression of learning with provisions for regular review and evaluations at prescribed stages of learning. The syllabus defines the unit of training, states by objective what the student is expected to accomplish during the unit of training, shows an organized plan for instruction, and dictates the evaluation process for either the unit or stages of learning.

transition training. An instructional program designed to familiarize and qualify a pilot to fly types of aircraft not previously flown such as tailwheel aircraft, high performance aircraft, and aircraft capable of flying at high altitudes.

very light jet (VLJ). Jet aircraft weighing 10,000 pounds or less maximum certificated takeoff weight and certificated for single pilot operations. These aircraft will possess at least some of the following features: 1) advanced cockpit automation, such as moving map GPS and multi-function displays; 2) automated engine and systems management; and 3) integrated autoflight, autopilot and flight-guidance systems.

Acronyms and Abbreviations Used in this Book

ALT	Altitude (as a function of the autopilot)
ATC	Air Traffic Control
CFI	Certificated Flight Instructor
CFIT	Controlled Flight Into Terrain
CRM	Cockpit Resource Management
CTA	Common Traffic Advisory Frequency
FAA	Federal Aviation Administration
FITS	FAA/Industry Training Standards
GPS	Global Positioning System
HDG	Heading (as a function of the autopilot)
LOFT	Line Oriented Flight Training
LOS	Line Oriented Simulation
MFD	Multi Function Display
MSL	Mean Sea Level
PFD	Primary Flight Display
PTS	Practical Test Standards
SBT	Scenario Based Training
SOP	Standard Operating Procedure
SRM	Single Pilot Resource Management
TAA	Technically Advanced Aircraft
VNAV	Vertical navigation

IFR General NTSB Reports

DEN01FA030: The airplane was on a full ILS approach to runway 18 at an airport with elevation 6,445 feet, in a mountainous area, at night. The control tower was closed. During non-tower operation hours, the airport used PCL on the tower frequency. The copilot made multiple attempts to turn on lights using the UNICOM frequency, which had been the CTAF until 6 months before. The captain continued his approach below IAP minimums without the runway lights being on. While in the landing flare, the captain reported that strong crosswinds and blowing snow created a "white-out" weather condition. The airplane touched down 195 feet left of the runway centerline in snow-covered terrain between the runway and taxiway. Two ILS 18 approach plates were found in the plane. One, out of date, showed UNICOM as the CTAF. The other was current and showed the tower frequency as CTAF. NTSB determines the probable cause(s) of this accident as: The pilot's failure to follow IFR approach procedures and perform a missed approach when the runway was not in sight below approach minimums. Contributing factors were the copilot's failure to follow current ILS approach procedures and use the correct frequency to turn on the runway lights, the snowy white-out conditions near the ground, and the dark night light conditions.

- Do you think that attempting to get the lights turned on was a distraction for the captain?
- Did that distraction possibly cause the descent below minimums?
- On approach, do you think the pilot was in radio communications with anyone?
- Could ATC have helped answer the question of why the lights were not on?
- What other equipment in the airplane do you have available to locate the proper frequencies?
- Would you land after an IAP if you couldn't get the lights turned on? At what point would you abort?
- This is also a lesson in resources management. When you need help, get it early.

ANC00LA029: The airplane collided with frozen pack ice, 3 miles from the airport, during a GPS IAP. Three-quarter-mile visibility, snow and fog were reported at the time of the accident. The pilot stated that he began a steep descent with the autopilot engaged. He indicated that as the airplane crossed the final approach course, the autopilot turned the airplane inbound toward the airport. He continued the steep descent, noted the airplane had overshot the course, and the autopilot was not correcting very well. He disengaged the autopilot and manually increased the correction heading to intercept the final approach course. During the descent he completed the landing checklist, extended the landing gear and flaps, and was tuning both the communications and navigation radios. The pilot said he looked up from tuning the radios to see the sea ice coming up too quickly to react, and impacted terrain. There were no pre-accident anomalies with the airplane. The NTSB determines the probable cause of this accident as: The pilot descended below the MDA. Factors associated with this accident were the task overload of the pilot during the instrument approach, and not performing a level off.

- Was this a stabilized approach?
- Why would a pilot perform a "steep" descent into an airport?
- At ¾ mile visibility, is there any room for any distractions or abnormal procedures?
- When would you have elected to abort the landing?
- What are your personal minimum for a "steep descent?"
- This is also a lesson in the accident chain. How many things went wrong for this pilot?

LAX03CA208: During an attempted go-around from a simulated emergency landing, the airplane failed to achieve a positive climb rate and descended to ground impact. After full power was added in order to abort the simulated emergency landing at 200 feet AGL, the student pitched the nose up and the airspeed began to decay as the airplane began sinking towards the terrain. The flaps, which had been in the full down position, were inadvertently retracted all at once. Both pilots agreed that the engine responded normally and that all flight controls functioned properly. The NTSB determines the probable cause(s) of this accident as: the student pilot's failure to maintain an adequate airspeed and his premature raising of the flaps during a go-around, which led to an inadvertent stall/mush. The flight instructor's inadequate supervision of the flight is also causal.

- The go-around was initiated at 200 AGL. Do pilots generally know within 200 AGL that a go-around is imminent?

- Is the go-around a procedure by the checklist or a procedure that is completed then confirmed with checklist?
- What is the implication of retracting flaps on the go-around?
- This is a lesson in always being mentally primed for a go-around procedure in every landing. Add it to your pre-landing checklist. Add the "Primed for Go-Around" thought process to your prelanding checklist.

LAX04CA130: The airplane departed the taxiway and collided with terrain while taxiing after landing. After taxiing off the runway, the controller cleared the pilot to taxi to the ramp. The pilot was unfamiliar with the airport and requested further instructions. In an effort to comply with what he thought the controller was telling him to do, he departed the taxiway. He continued down a grassy area and collided with a median. The pilot reported no pre-impact mechanical malfunctions with the airplane. The NTSB determines the probable cause(s) of this accident as: the pilot's inadequate visual lookout, which resulted in his failure to maintain proper alignment with the taxiway. Factors in the accident were dusk lighting conditions and pilot not understanding the ground control taxi clearance.

- What tools should a pilot use when unfamiliar with the airport?
- Was the pilot on the taxiway centerline?
- When following progressive taxi clearances, is there ever an instance when you would taxi into the grass?
- This is a lesson in communications. At what point and what conditions would you question and/or confirm a controller's clearance?

NYC01FA058: Pilot and passenger departed on a night IFR flight. Weather en route was a mix of IMC and VMC. When the airplane was 17 SW of its destination, the pilot was cleared for an IAP. At 9 miles, the pilot reported the airport in sight, and canceled IFR. The airplane continued to descend towards the airport on a modified left base until radar contact was lost at 3,300 feet MSL. The pilot was in radio contact with his wife just prior to the accident. He advised her that he was on base for runway 32. Neither the pilot's wife, nor ATC, received a distress call from the pilot. The airplane was located the next morning. The accident site was 7.9 miles from the airport and 1,200 feet above airport elevation. Light snow showers were in the vicinity and satellite imagery showed that the airplane was operating under a solid overcast.

The NTSB determines the probable cause(s) of this accident as: The PICs failure to maintain sufficient altitude while maneuvering to land which resulted in a collision with terrain. Factors in the accident were the dark night, mountainous terrain, snow showers, clouds, and the pilot's decision to cancel his IFR clearance.

- Does carrying passengers affect pilot decisions for continuing an approach?
- Which do you think is riskier – VMC, IMC or a mix?
- What is the implication of canceling IFR before short final? Why would you do that? Why not?
- What is the implication of talking to his wife on the radio? Was this a distraction for the pilot?
- What is the difference between remaining IFR and remaining on the IAP?
- This is a lesson in following procedures. What is your personal policy regarding leaving an IAP procedure?
- What is your personal policy about knowing the MSA during approach?

MIA99FA168: During taxi and takeoff on runway 9R, pilot and passengers stated the windows of the aircraft were fogged due to rain. The passengers could not see out the front windows. The pilot stated he could see out the front windows. The passengers also stated the pilot was holding the control wheel full to the right during takeoff. The winds were reported to be from 030 at 10 knots. During takeoff roll the aircraft drifted to the left and went off the runway. The aircraft then crossed over a taxiway and collided with a taxiway identifier sign. No windshear alerts were recorded and no standing water was observed on the runway. The NTSB determines the probable cause(s) of this accident as: The pilot's takeoff with condensation on the cockpit windows which restricted visibility, his improper use of aileron control, improper compensation for winds, and his failure to maintain directional control during takeoff.

- How do you correct fog on the windows? How else?
- Why couldn't the passengers see out the front windows when the pilot could?
- Taking off from runway 9 with winds from 030—would we ordinarily expect the airplane to go off the runway to the left in such a crosswind?
- Do you think the restricted window visibility was a distraction for the pilot?

- We can't argue NTSB findings, but does anything else come to your mind that may have caused this accident?

MIA04CA005: During takeoff and when the pilot was about one-quarter of the distance from the end of the runway he attempted to pull back on the control yoke and lift off, but nothing happened. He noticed the airspeed was about 60 knots, but yet he could not raise the nose of the airplane, so he applied the brakes in an attempt to stop, and the airplane departed off the end of the runway. He did not remove the control lock prior to flight, and added that prior to the accident there were no mechanical malfunctions. The NTSB determines the probable cause(s) of this accident as: The pilot's improper preflight planning which resulted in the airplane's gust lock being left installed.

- Any pilot can make a mistake; this is a lesson in the redundancy built into our system to catch mistakes.
- Did the pilot perform a preflight inspection?
- Did the pilot use his checklist for "Controls Free and Correct"?
- Do you think the pilot used ANY checklist carefully?
- Why do you think that is? (complacency, feeling rushed)

CHI04CA095: The airplane sustained substantial damage when it exited the runway during an aborted landing. The instructor reported, "The aircraft turned final and flew a slightly low and fast approach to the runway. The aircraft touched down flat on the runway and because of the excess speed the aircraft bounced into the air a considerable amount. As the power was advanced for go-around, the aircraft began a left turn and drifted off the runway. At this point the instructor called for complete control of the aircraft and returned to wings-level pitch attitude; however, despite the application of full power the aircraft refused to climb and touched down right main first on the grass to the north side of the runway. An examination of the wreckage revealed that the flight controls were correct and that engine controls were operational. The NTSB determines the probable cause(s) of this accident as: The student pilot not maintaining airplane control during the go-around and the flight instructor's inadequate remedial action.

- What is a stabilized approach?
- The instructor talks about "the aircraft turned…" Who is responsible for what the airplane does?
- What is "slightly low" is there ever an altitude in your mind that you are satisfied with "slightly low"?

- Why did the airplane touchdown "flat?"
- Why did the airplane turn left on the go-around?

ATL04CA129: Prior to departing on the return flight, the CFI checked Internet weather, and observed "bad weather" approaching the departure airport. He and the student departed from runway 25 performing a soft-field takeoff. Immediately after rotation, the CFI leveled the airplane to increase airspeed. The CFI stated, "This took longer than usual due to wind shear." The airplane reached 60 knots and they were between 25 to 50 feet on initial takeoff climb, when they encountered a "severe crosswind gust of an estimated 40 to 50 knots from the right putting the wings in a near vertical attitude." The CFI applied rudder and aileron, and the airplane collided with the trees and the ground. Another pilot who landed at the airport before the accident-airplane departed stated, black clouds were visible in the distance. The NTSB determines the probable cause(s) of this accident as: The CFI initiated flight into thunderstorm activity.

- What does "black clouds" indicate to you?
- What is the risk in rushing for takeoff ahead of "bad weather?"
- How do you feel about the pilot's choice of a soft-field takeoff within this situation?
- Aerodynamically, was there a better choice of takeoffs in consideration of "bad weather?"
- Was the pilot over the runway centerline when the gust was encountered?

CHI02LA111: The air carrier passenger flight encountered severe turbulence while in cruise. Three passengers were seriously injured, while nine passengers and three flight attendants received minor injuries during the turbulence. The airplane was traveling at 37,000 feet altitude. Weather products showed extreme intensity thunderstorms existed in the area. Weather data and aircraft position radar data show that the airplane was 9 miles S–SW of a cloud buildup that extended to 39,000 feet. Additionally, the airplane was 5 miles west of an extreme intensity radar echo associated with the thunderstorms in the area. No National Weather Service aviation weather advisories were in effect for the location and time of the turbulence encounter. Communications transcripts show that the flight crew requested and were granted a course deviation for weather about 10 minutes prior to the upset. However, the Digital Flight Data Recorder shows that the seat belt sign was illuminated only 10 seconds prior to the encounter. The NTSB determines the probable cause(s) of this accident as: The flight crew's failure to follow weather avoidance procedures and their delay in activating the seat belt sign. Factors were the turbulent thunderstorm weather conditions, and the failure of the National Weather Service to issue an applicable in-flight weather advisory.

- Is a 39,000-foot thunderstorm robust? What would you expect for turbulence around this cell?
- What is the risk of flying at an altitude near the top of the thunderstorm?
- Okay, so you don't normally fly at 39,000 feet. But, aerodynamically, what is the implication of flying near the upper limits of any aircraft service ceiling in the turbulence?

ANC04LA009: The flight was on an IAP in dark night conditions to the destination airport when it collided with a tree. The flight was able to continue and land at the destination airport without further incident. The flight crew was cleared for the LDA-2 approach to runway 8, and were inside the FAF when the collision occurred. The LDA-2 approach MDA is 1,000 feet, and the distance from the FAF to the touchdown zone is 3.2 miles. The weather at the destination airport at the time of arrival was 2 miles visibility, in light snow, with an 800-foot obscured ceiling. He said the tree that was struck by the airplane was about 2 miles from the airport, and .24 miles north of the course centerline. The inspector said the tree's base elevation was between 200 to 300 feet MSL, and he estimated the tree's height at 100 feet AGL. The NTSB determines the probable cause(s) of this accident as: The pilot's failure to maintain altitude/clearance from obstacles when approaching the airport. Factors associated with the accident were the dark night, snow showers, and the pilot's failure to maintain runway alignment.

- Would a clear night with a moon have helped the pilot see the tree? Would he have been looking?
- What is an LDA? An LDA-2?
- Do you suppose this was the best choice of IAPs? Did he consider others?
- The MDA is 1,000 – is that MSL or AGL? The ceiling is 800 – is this MSL or AGL?
- Is 800/2 within your personal flight minimums?
- .24 miles off centerline, 2 miles away…how many dots on the CDI do you think he was off?
- This is a lesson in CFIT.

Bibliography

Listed by chapter, then alphabetically by author or source document. Some of the resources below are available online; see listing of website addresses beginning on Page 211.

Chapter 1:

Dillman, B., Lee, J. (2006) "Utilizing Situational Judgment Tests for Pilot Decision Making." FAA Academy. *International Journal of Applied Aviation Studies,* Volume 6, Number 1.

Jensen, Richard. (July 1988) *Aeronautical Decision Making for Commercial Pilots.* Federal Aviation Administration. DOT/FAA/PM-86-42. Available from National Technical Information Service, Springfield, VA. as ADA198772. www.NTIS.gov

McMahon, Arlynn (2005). *Making a Complete Pilot.* National Association of Flight Instructors. *Mentor Magazine*

NASA Conference Publication 2184, *Guidelines for Line-Oriented Flight Training,* Volume I, National Aeronautics and Space Administration Scientific and Technical Information Branch 1981.

Chapter 2:

Betrand, John. (2005) *"Practices of High-Time Instructors in Part 61 Environments. FAA Academy."* International Journal of Applied Aviation Studies, Volume 5, Number 1.

Betrand, J. (2005) "Decision Making and Judgment." FAA Academy. *International Journal of Applied Aviation Studies,* Volume 5, Number 2.

Bustamante, E., Fallon, C., Bliss J., Bailey, W., Anderson, B. (2005) "Pilot's Workload, Situation Awareness and Trust During Weather Events as a Function of Time, Pressure, Role Assignment, Pilot's Rank, Weather Display and Weather System." FAA Academy. *International Journal of Applied Aviation Studies,* Volume 5, Number 2, p. 352

Castner, S., Heraldez, D., and Jones, K. (2006) "Retention of Aeronautical Knowledge." FAA Academy. *International Journal of Applied Aviation Studies,* Volume 6, Number 1.

FAA1. Practical Risk Management for Local VFR Flying.

FAA2. Practical Risk Management for VFR XC Flying.

FAA3. Practical Risk Management for Night VFR Flying.

FAA4. *Tips for Teaching Practical Risk Management.*

FAA5. *Introduction to Pilot Judgment.* FAA Accident Prevention Program. FAA-P-8740-53. AFS-21-0491.

Hunter, David, *Aviation Human Factors* website, www.avhf.com. Go to: http://www.avhf.com/html/Evaluation/PilotJudgment/Pilot_Judgment_Movie.htm

Hunter, David (2003) "Measuring G/A Pilot Judgment Using a Situational Judgment Technique." FAA. *The International Journal of Aviation Psychology* 13(4) 373-386

Jensen, Richard. (July 1988) *Aeronautical Decision Making for Commercial Pilots.* (ibid.)

Knecht, W., Harris, H., Shappell, S. (April 2005) "The influence of Visibility, Cloud Ceiling, Financial Incentive and Personality Factors on General Aviation Pilot's Willingness to Takeoff into Marginal Weather," Part I. DOT/FAA/AM-05/7. Civil Aerospace Medical Institute, FAA. Oklahoma City, OK.

Chapter 3:

CFI. FITS Flight Instructor Training Module I. Federal Aviation Administration.

CFI-2. FITS Flight Instructor Training Module. Volume 2. Federal Aviation Administration. *System Safety Course Developers Guide.* (For inclusion in FAA-Approved FIRCs.)

Dismukes, R., Jobe, K., and McDonnell, L. (1997) *Facilitating LOFT Debriefings: Instructor Techniques and Crew Participation.*

FAA (1991) *Aeronautical Decision Making* (Advisory Circular 60-22).

FITS. (February 2006) *FITS Curriculum Acceptance Criteria.* V.2. Federal Aviation Administration.

Fitzpatrick, John (1990) *Technical Education—Working with the System* (FSF).

Foushee, Clayton H. (January 23-25, 1989). *Preparing for the Unexpected: A Psychologist's Case for Improved Training.* NASA. Presented at the International Airline Pilot Training Seminar, Caracas, Venezuela.

Hunter, David (2003) "Measuring G/A Pilot Judgment Using a Situational Judgment Technique." *The International Journal of Aviation Psychology* 13(4) 373-386

Maryland Department of Education.

Master Instructor Syllabus. *TAA Scenario Based Instructor's Guide.* (2006, June) Federal Aviation Administration. Version 2.0.

SBT. Course Developers Guide. (September 2005) Federal Aviation Administration.

Chapter 4:

Diehl, A., Hwoschinsky, P., Lawton, R., Livack, G. (May 1982) ADM. *Aeronautical Decision Making for Students and Pilots.* DOT/FAA PM-86/41. National Technical Information System, Springfield, VA ADA182549

Dismukes, R., Jobe, K., McDonnell, L., and Smith, G. What is Facilitation and Why Use It? In R.K. Dismukes and G.M. Smith (eds.) *Facilitation and a Debriefing in Aviation Training and Operations* (p 1-12) Aldershot, UK: Ashgate.

Dismukes, R., Jobe, K., and McDonnell, L. (1997) *Facilitating LOFT Debriefings: Instructor Techniques and Crew Participation.*

FAA (1999) *Aviation Instructor's Handbook.* FAA-H-8083-9. Federal Aviation Administration

FAA (1990). Line Operational Simulations (Advisory Circular 120-35B). Washington, DC

FITS LCG Learner Centered Grading.

McDonnell, L., Jobe, K., and Dismukes, R. (November 1997) Facilitating LOS Debriefings: A Training Manual. *Flight Safety Digest,* Vol 16, No. 11. Flight Safety Foundation

Chapter 5:

FSF (July 2005) VLJ. Flight Safety Digest. Flight Safety Foundation

GAO. (1999, July) Aviation Safety: Research Supports Limited Use of Personal Computer Aviation Training Devices for Pilots (Letter Report GAO/RCED-99-143).

Saleem, J. and Kleiner, B. (2005). The Effects of Nighttime and Deteriorating Visual Conditions on Pilot Performance, Workload and Situation Awareness in General Aviation for both VFR and IFR Approaches. *International Journal of Applied Aviation Studies,* 5, Number 1. FAA Academy.

Taylor, H., Talleur, D., Emanuel, A., Rantanen, E. (2005) Transfer of Training Effectiveness of a Flight Training Device (FTD). Presented at the 13th International Symposium on Aviation Psychology, Dayton, OH.

Chapter 6:

AOPA. (2006) Single Pilot IFR. AOPA Safety Advisor.

Castner, S., Heraldez, D., and Jones, K. (2006) Retention of Aeronautical Knowledge. FAA Academy. *International Journal of Applied Aviation Studies*, Volume 6, Number 1.

CFR. Code of Federal Regulations 61.56.

Jensen, Richard. (July 1988) *Aeronautical Decision Making for Commercial Pilots* (ibid.)

PTS (April 2004) *Instrument Rating Practical Test Standards for Airplane Helicopter and Powered Lift.* FAA-S-8081-4D. Federal Aviation Administration.

Chapter 7:

FAA. (1999) *Aviation Instructor's Handbook.* FAA-H-8083-9. Federal Aviation Administration.

Jensen, Richard (July 1988) *Aeronautical Decision Making for Commercial Pilots* (ibid.)

Chapter 8:

Batt, R., O'Hare, D. (June 2005) General Aviation Pilot Behaviors in the Face of Adverse Weather. *Australian Transport Safety Bureau.* B2005/0127

Burian, Barbara K., Ph.D. (September 2002) *General Aviation Pilot Weather Knowledge and Training*

COPA. Cirrus Owners and Pilots Association. Available at www.copa. org (Membership required.)

FITS. (October 2003) *Personal and Weather Risk Assessment Guide* Version 1.0. FAA/Industry Training Standards

Foushee, H.Clayton. Preparing for the Unexpected: A Psychologist's Case for Improved Training. Presented at the International Airline Pilot Training Seminar, Caracas, Venezuela on January 23, 1989.

Hunter, D., Martinussen, M., and Wiggins, M. (2003) Understanding How

Pilots Make Weather-Related Decisions. *The International Journal of Aviation Psychology,* 13(1), 73–87 Lawrence Erlbaum Associates, Inc.

Knecht, W., Harris, H., Shappell, S. (April 2005) The Influence of Visibility, Cloud Ceiling, Financial Incentive and Personality Factors on General Aviation Pilot's Willingness to Takeoff into Marginal Weather Part I. DOT/FAA/AM-05/7. Civil Aerospace Medical Institute, FAA. Oklahoma City, OK.

Wiegmann, Douglas and Go, Juliana. (November 2000). VFR Flight into Adverse Weather: An Empirical Investigation of Factors Affecting Pilot Decision Making. Aviation Research Lab Institute of Aviation. FAA Technical Report ARL-00-15/FAA-00-8.

Chapter 9:

Diehl, Alan; Hwoschinsky, Peter; Livak, Gary; Lawton, Russell. (May 1987) *Aeronautical Decision Making for Student and Private Pilots.* DOT/FAA/PM-86/41. Available from National Technical Information Service, www.ntis.gov.

FAA (1999) *Aviation Instructors Handbook.* FAA-H-8083-9.

FAA. Introduction to Pilot Judgment. FAA Accident Prevention Program. FAA-P-8740-53. AFS-21-0491.

Hunter, David, *Aviation Human Factors website* (ibid.)

Jensen, R., Adrion, J., Lawton, R. (May 1987) *Aeronautical Decision Making for Instrument Pilots.* DOT/FAA/PM-86/43. Available from National Technical Information Service, www.ntis.gov.

Discipline. *Professional Safety.* (Author unknown.) Personal website.

Chapter 10:

NTSB (National Transportation Safety Board) Database.

210. *Survey of NTSB accidents.*

Seneca. *Survey of NTSB accidents.*

NASA. Aviation Safety Reporting System. Administered by NASA.

Chapter 11:

Baker, D. and Dismukes, R. (2003) *A Gold Standards Approach to Training Instructors to Evaluate Crew Performance.* NASA Technical Memorandum 212809. Moffett Field, CA.

Chapter 12:

AOPA Magazine. Aircraft Owners and Pilot's Association. Available at www.aopa.org (Membership required.)

Batt, R., O'Hare, D. (June 2005) (ibid.)

Butler, Roy. LOFT Design Focus Group Report. NASA/UT. CRM Industry Workshop.

CAP 720 (2002, August). Flight Crew Training: Cockpit Resource Management (CRM) and Line-Oriented Flight Training (LOFT) (previously ICAO Digest No. 2)

Flying Magazine. Available at www.flyingmag.com (Subscription required.)

Jensen, R., Guilkey, J., and Hunter, D. (February 1998) An Evaluation of Pilot Acceptance of the Personal Minimums Training Program for Risk Management. FAA DOT/FAA/AM-98/6.

Training Guidelines for Single Pilot Operations of Very Light Jets and Technically Advanced Aircraft. (January 2005) *National Business Aviation Association.*

Chapter 13:

Betrand, John (2005) (ibid.).

Dismukes, R. (July 2000) *Rethinking Crew Error: Overview of a Panel Session.*

Geller, Scott. (May 2000) "Does feeling safe make us more reckless?" Article retrieved 12/10/06 from *Industrial Safety & Hygiene News* magazine website.

Veillette, Pat, Ph.D. (November 2006) *Loss of Control.* Book Surge, LLC.

Wilde, G.J.S. *Accident models: Risk homeostasis.* Chapter 56.10 in Jeanne. M. Stellman (Editor-in-Chief), *ILO Encyclopeadia of Occupational Health and Safety* (4th edition). Geneva, Switzerland: International Labour Office, 1998.

Online Resources Used in *Train Like You Fly*
Internet addresses, listed by chapter.

Chapter 1
Dillman, B., Lee, J. (2006) "Utilizing Situational Judgment Tests for Pilot Decision Making." FAA Academy. *International Journal of Applied Aviation Studies,* Volume 6, Number 1. Available at: **http://www.journal.faa.gov/ pdfs%20and%20native%20files/IJAAS%20SP-2006%20for%20web.pdf**

Chapter 2
Betrand, John. (2005) "Practices of High-Time Instructors in Part 61 Environments. FAA Academy." *International Journal of Applied Aviation Studies,* Volume 5, Number 1. Available at: **http://www.journal.faa.gov/ pdfs%20and%20native%20files/Fall2005WebEdition.pdf**

Betrand, J. (2005) "Decision Making and Judgment." FAA Academy. *International Journal of Applied Aviation Studies,* Volume 5, Number 2. Available at: **http://www.journal.faa.gov/pdfs%20and%20native%20files /Fall2005WebEdition.pdf**

Castner, S., Heraldez, D., and Jones, K. (2006) "Retention of Aeronautical Knowledge." FAA Academy. *International Journal of Applied Aviation Studies,* Volume 6, Number 1. Available at: **http:// www.journal.faa.gov/pdfs%20and%20native%20files/IJAAS%20SP- 2006%20for%20web.pdf**

FAA1. Practical Risk Management for Local VFR Flying. Available at: **http://www.faa.gov/library/manuals/pilot_risk/media/ 2.0%20Local%20VFR.pdf**

FAA2. Practical Risk Management for VFR XC Flying. Available at: **http:// www.faa.gov/library/manuals/pilot_risk/media/3.0%20VFR%20XC.pdf**

FAA3. Practical Risk Management for Night VFR Flying. Available at: **http://www.faa.gov/library/manuals/pilot_risk/media/ 4.0%20Night%20VFR.pdf**

FAA4. *Tips for Teaching Practical Risk Management.* Available at: **http://www.faa.gov/library/manuals/pilot_risk/media/ 1.0%20Practical%20Risk%20Management.pdf**

Chapter 3

CFI. FITS Flight Instructor Training Module I. Federal Aviation Administration. Retrieved December 1, 2006. Available at: **http://www. faa.gov/education_research/training/fits/training/flight_instructor/ media/Volum1.pdf**

CFI-2. FITS Flight Instructor Training Module. Volume 2. Federal Aviation Administration. System Safety Course Developers Guide. For Inclusion in FAA-Approved Flight Instructor Refresher Clinics. Retrieved December 1, 2006. Available at: **http://www.faa.gov/ education_research/training/fits/training/flight_instructor/media/ Volume2.pdf**

Dismukes, R., Jobe, K., and McDonnell, L. (1997) Facilitating LOFT Debriefings: Instructor Techniques and Crew Participation. Downloaded November 2, 2006. Available at: **http://human-factors.arc.nasa.gov/ihs/flightcognition/Publications/ IJAP.pdf**

FITS. (2006, February) FITS Curriculum Acceptance Criteria. V.2. Federal Aviation Administration. Retrieved December 1, 2006. Available at: **http://www.faa.gov/education_research/training/fits/ guidance/media/criteria.pdf**

Master Instructor Syllabus. *TAA Scenario Based Instructor's Guide.* (2006, June) Federal Aviation Administration. Version 2.0. Retrieved December 1, 2006. Available at: **http://www.faa.gov/education_research/training/ fits/training/generic/media/instructor.pdf**

SBT. Course Developers Guide. (September 2005) Federal Aviation Administration. Retrieved December 1, 2006. Available at: **http://www. faa.gov/education_research/training/fits/training/generic/media/ course_developers.pdf**

Chapter 4

Dismukes, R., Jobe, K., McDonnell, L., and Smith, G. What is Facilitation and Why Use It? In R.K. Dismukes and G.M. Smith (eds.) *Facilitation and a Debriefing in Aviation Training and Operations* (p 1-12) Aldershot UK: Ashgate. Downloaded November 2, 2006. Available at: **http://human-factors.arc.nasa.gov/ihs/flightcognition/Publications/ChapterOne.pdf**

Dismukes, R., Jobe, K., and McDonnell, L. (1997) Facilitating LOFT Debriefings: Instructor Techniques and Crew Participation. Downloaded November 2, 2006. Available at: http://human-factors.arc.nasa.gov/ihs/flightcognition/Publications/IJAP.pdf

FITS LCG Learner Centered Grading. Available at: http://www.faa.gov/education_research/training/fits/guidance/media/lcg.pdf

McDonnell, L., Jobe, K., and Dismukes, R. (November 1997,) Facilitating LOS Debriefings: A Training Manual. Flight Safety Digest, Vol 16, No. 11. *Flight Safety Foundation.* Retrieved November 10, 2006. Available at: http://www.flightsafety.org_members_serveme.cfm_path=fsd_fsd_nov97

Chapter 5

GAO. (1999, July) Aviation Safety: Research Supports Limited Use of Personal Computer Aviation Training Devices for Pilots (Letter Report GAO/RCED-99-143). Downloaded November 1, 2006, Available at: http://www.faa.gov/safety/programs_initiatives/aircraft_aviation/nsp/flight_training/qualification_process/media/GAO_PCATD.txt

Saleem, J. and Kleiner, B. (2005). The Effects of Nighttime and Deteriorating Visual Conditions on Pilot Performance, Workload and Situation Awareness in General Aviation for both VFR and IFR Approaches. *International Journal of Applied Aviation Studies,* 5, Number 1. FAA Academy. Downloaded November 10, 2006. Available at: http://www.journal.faa.gov/pdfs%20and%20native%20files/JournalSpring2005%20v3.pdf

Taylor, H., Talleur, D., Emanuel, A., Rantanen, E. (2005) Transfer of Training Effectiveness of a Flight Training Device (FTD). Presented at the 13th International Symposium on Aviation Psychology, Dayton, OH. Downloaded November 15, 2006. Available at: http://www.humanfactors.uiuc.edu/Reports&PapersPDFs/isap05/taytalemaranavpsy05.pdf

Chapter 6

AOPA. (2006) Single Pilot IFR. AOPA Safety Advisor. Downloaded November 15, 2006. Available at: http://www.aopa.org/asf/publications/sa05.pdf

Castner, S., Heraldez, D., and Jones, K. (2006) Retention of Aeronautical Knowledge. FAA Academy. International Journal of Applied Aviation Studies, Volume 6, Number 1. Available at: **http://www.journal.faa.gov/pdfs%20and%20native%20files/IJAAS%20SP-2006%20for%20web.pdf**

CFR. Code of Federal Regulations 61.56. Downloaded December 15, 2006. Available at: **http://ecfr.gpoaccess.gov**

PTS (April 2004) INSTRUMENT RATING Practical Test Standards for AIRPLANE HELICOPTER and POWERED LIFT. FAA-S-8081-4D. Federal Aviation Administration. Downloaded December 1, 2006. Available at: **http://www.faa.gov/education_research/testing/airmen/test_standards/media/FAA-S-8081-4D.pdf**

Chapter 8

Batt, R., O'Hare, D. (June 2005) General Aviation Pilot Behaviors in the Face of Adverse Weather. *Australian Transport Safety Bureau.* B2005/0127 Available at: **http://www.atsb.gov.au**

Burian, Barbara K., Ph.D. (September 2002) *General Aviation Pilot Weather Knowledge and Training* Retrieved October 17, 2006 from: **http://www.avhf.com/html/Publications/Tech_Reports/CFI%20Survey%20Final%20Report.pdf**

FITS. (October 2003) *Personal and Weather Risk Assessment Guide* Version 1.0. FAA/Industry Training Standards. Available at: **http://www.faa.gov/education_research/training/fits/guidance/media/Pers%20Wx%20Risk%20Assessment%20Guide-V1.0.pdf**

Foushee, H. Clayton. Preparing for the Unexpected: A Psychologist's Case for Improved Training. Presented at the International Airline Pilot Training Seminar, Caracas, Venezuela on January 23, 1989. Retrieved September 31, 2006 from: **http://www.flightsafety.org/members/serveme.cfm?path=fsd/fsd_mar90.pdf**

Hunter D, Martinussen M, Wiggins M. (2003) Understanding How Pilots Make Weather-Related Decisions. *The International Journal of Aviation Psychology, 13*(1), 73–87 Lawrence Erlbaum Associates, Inc. Retrieved November 15, 2006. Available at: **http://www.avhf.com/html/Publications/Tech_Reports/IJAP%20Wx%20Decisions.pdf** (Membership required.)

Wiegmann, Douglas and Go, Juliana. (November 2000). VFR Flight into Adverse Weather: An Empirical Investigation of Factors Affecting Pilot

Decision Making. *Aviation Research Lab Institute of Aviation. FAA Technical Report* ARL-00-15/FAA-00-8. Retrieved October 18, 2006 from: **http://www.humanfactors.uiuc.edu/Reports&PapersPDFs/TechReport/00-15.pdf** (Membership required.)

Chapter 9

Discipline. *Professional Safety.* (Author unknown.) Downloaded November 2006. Available at: **http://www.btinternet.com/~hftk/HFTK_1_Core_HF/Pesonal_Qualities/Briefing_Notes_Discipline_v2.doc**

Chapter 11

Baker, D. and Dismukes, R. (2003). *A Gold Standards Approach to Training Instructors to Evaluate Crew Performance.* (NASA Technical Memorandum 212809). Moffett Field, CA: Downloaded November 2006. Available at: **http://human-factors.arc.nasa.gov/flightcognition/Publications/GoldStandardsTM.PDFA**

Chapter 12

CAP 720 (August 2002). Flight Crew Training: Cockpit Resource Management (CRM) and Line-Oriented Flight Training (LOFT). (previously ICAO Digest No. 2) Retrieved from: **http://www.caa.co.uk.**

Jensen, R., Guilkey, J., and Hunter, D. (February 1998) An Evaluation of Pilot Acceptance of the Personal Minimums Training Program for Risk Management. FAA DOT/FAA/AM-98/6. Available at: **http://www.avhf.com/html/Publications/Tech_Reports/FAA%20Report%20Evaluation%20of%20program%20for%20risk%20management.pdf**

Chapter 13

Betrand, John E. (2005) Practices of High-Time Instructors in Part 61 Environments. FAA Academy. *International Journal of Applied Aviation Studies, Volume* 5, Number 1. Available at: **http://www.journal.faa.gov/pdfs%20and%20native%20files/Fall2005WebEdition.pdf**

Dismukes, R. (July 2000) *Rethinking Crew Error: Overview of a Panel Session* Downloaded November 2006. Available at: **http://human-factors.arc.nasa.gov/flightcognition/Publications/KD_Panel_ISAP01_417.pdf**

Geller, S. (May 2000) "Does feeling safe make us more reckless?" Retrieved from **http://www.ishn.com/CDA/Articles/Behavioral_Safety/5d5d1959d8fb7010VgnVCM100000f932a8c0**

Footnotes Listed by Chapter

Chapter 1: Concepts
1. McMahon, 2005, Making a Complete Pilot.
2. Jensen, 1988, p. i
3. Dillman, Lee, 2006, p. 146
4. Dillman, Lee, 2006, p. 145

Chapter 2: Making a Good Pilot
1. Jensen, 1988, p. 1
2. Bertrand, John, 2005, p. 41
3. ibid., p. 379
4. From "Aviation Human Factors" website, D. Hunter
5. Adapted from Hunter, David (2003)
6. ibid.
7. Castner, S., Heraldez, D., and Jones, K., 2006, p. 95
8. Knecht, W., Harris, H., Shappell, S., April 2005, p. 13

Chapter 3: Syllabus Redesign
1. Dismukes, Jobe, and McDonnell; 1997, p. 4
2. Hunter
3. Foushee, 1989
4. CFI, p.3; p. 7
5. CFI-2, p. 12; p.1
6. FITS, p. 1

Chapter 4: Debriefing and Evaluating
1. FAA Advisory Circular 120-35C, Line Operational Simulations (2004)
2. Dismukes, Jobe, and McDonnell, 1997
3. ADM, p. 5
4. Dismukes, McDonnel, Jobe, and Smith, What is Facilitation and Why Use it?
5. Adapted from Facilitating LOS Debriefings: A Training Manual (1997)

Chapter 5: Instrument Scenario Training
 1. Henry, Talleur, Emanuel and Rantanen, 2005, p. 4
 2. Saleem, J. and Kleiner, B., 2005

Chapter 6: Advanced Training Scenarios
 1. AOPA, 2006 p. 2
 2. AOPA, 2006 p. 9
 3. Castner, S., Heraldez, D., and Jones, K., 2006

Chapter 7: Scenarios for Fight Instructor Training
 1. FAA-H-8083-9, Page 5-10
 2. Loosely adapted from Jenson, Richard (1988) Aeronautical
    Decision Making for Commercial Pilots, p. 57
 3. Ibid., p.58

Chapter 8: Weather in Scenarios
 1. Burian, "CFI Weather Training Survey", from General Aviation
    Pilot Weather Knowledge and Training (FAA Grant #00-G-
    020), 2002
 2. Hunter, Martinussen, Wiggins, 2003, p. 75
 3. Batt and O'Hare, 2005, pp. 51, 55
 4. Ibid., and Knecht, W., Harris, H., Shappell, S., April 2005, p. 12
 5. Batt and O'Hare, 2005, p.52
 6. Hunter, Martinussen, Wiggins, 2003, p. 74

Chapter 9: The Right Attitude
 1. FAA, Aviation Instructors Handbook 1999, p. 9-14
 2. Scenarios adapted from Aeronautical Decision Making for
    Instrument Pilots
 3. Discipline, p. 1

Chapter 10: Wisdom Report Scenarios
 1. Adapted from NTSB, ANC03LA125
 2. NASA ASRA ACN:613230